Inclusive Middle Schools

Inclusive Middle Schools

by

Craig H. Kennedy, Ph.D.
Vanderbilt University
Nashville, Tennessee

and

Douglas Fisher, Ph.D.
San Diego State University
San Diego, California

with invited contributors

·P A U L·H·
BROOKES
PUBLISHING C⁹ ®

Baltimore • London • Sydney

Paul H. Brookes Publishing Co.
Post Office Box 10624
Baltimore, Maryland 21285-0624

www.brookespublishing.com

Typeset by Integrated Publishing Solutions, Grand Rapids, Michigan.
Manufactured in the United States of America by Versa Press, East Peoria, Illinois.

The names of the middle schools discussed in this book have been changed
to preserve the confidentiality of the middle schools and the individuals
associated with them. For the same reason, teachers' affiliations and
addresses have been omitted from the authors' and contributors' listings
at the front of this book.

Purchasers of this book may download free of charge from the Brookes
Publishing web site the usable forms. These forms are available at the
following address: www.brookespublishing.com/imsforms. Use of
these forms is granted for educational purposes only; the duplication
and distribution of these forms for a fee is prohibited.

Permission to use the following is gratefully acknowledged:

Cover illustration and chapter opener graphics copyright © 1998 by
Brian "Bydee Man" Joseph (www.Bydee.com).

Graphics/images on page 58, Figure 4.4, courtesy of ClickArt® Incredible
Image Pak™, copyright © 1996 The Learning Company, Inc., and its
subsidiaries. All rights reserved. Used by permission. ClickArt, Image Pak,
and Brøderbund are trademarks and/or registered trademarks of Learning
Company Properties, Inc.

Second printing, December 2003.

Library of Congress Cataloging-in-Publication Data

Kennedy, Craig H.
  Inclusive middle schools / by Craig H. Kennedy and Douglas Fisher.
     p.   cm.
  Includes bibliographical references and index.
  ISBN 1-55766-486-2
  1. Inclusive education.   2. Middle schools.   I. Fisher, Douglas (Douglas B.)
II. Title.
LC1200.K46   2001
371.9'046—dc21   00-046792
British Library Cataloguing in Publication data are available from the British
Library.

Contents

About the Authors vii
About the Contributors ix
Foreword   *Mara Sapon-Shevin* xi
To Our Readers xv
Acknowledgments xxi

1   Parallels Between the Problems and Possibilities
     in Contemporary Education
     Ian Pumpian, Douglas Fisher, and Craig H. Kennedy 1

I   **School Structures**

2   Administrative Leadership
     Craig H. Kennedy 17

3   Building and Using Collaborative School Teams
     Craig H. Kennedy and Douglas Fisher 27

II   **Inclusive Middle School Curriculum**

4   Access to the Middle School Core Curriculum
     Douglas Fisher and Craig H. Kennedy 43

5   Differentiated Instruction for Diverse
     Middle School Students
     Douglas Fisher and Craig H. Kennedy 61

6   Linking Assessment to Accountability and Instruction
     Douglas Fisher and Craig H. Kennedy 73

III **Student Supports**

7   Using Technology to Support
     Belonging and Achievement
     Caren Sax 89

8   Positive Behavior Support
     Craig H. Kennedy and Douglas Fisher 105

9   Tying It Together: Personal Supports that Lead
     to Membership and Belonging
     Nancy Frey 119

References 139

Index 149

About the Authors

Craig H. Kennedy, Ph.D., is Associate Professor in the Department of Special Education at Vanderbilt University in Nashville, Tennessee. He received his doctorate in 1992 from the University of California, Santa Barbara. Dr. Kennedy's interests are in social relationship development, approaches to effective teaching, strategies for effective inclusion in general education, and the social and biological causes of problem behavior. He has published more than 80 articles and book chapters on these and related issues and has served on the editorial boards of several journals related to education and psychology.

Douglas Fisher, Ph.D., is Associate Professor in the Department of Teacher Education at San Diego State University and has taught a range of courses in the teacher-credentialing program as well as graduate- and doctoral-level courses in the College of Education at San Diego State University. Dr. Fisher teaches classes in English language development and literacy. His background includes adolescent literacy and instructional strategies for students with diverse needs. He often presents at local, state, and national conferences and has published a number of articles on reading/literacy, differentiated instruction, accommodations, and curriculum.

About the Contributors

Nancy Frey, M.A., is a faculty member at San Diego State University, teaching preservice teachers in reading and language arts, classroom management, and instructional practices. She also serves as a consultant on inclusive education to the Florida Inclusion Network.

Ian Pumpian, Ph.D., is Professor in Educational Leadership at San Diego State University and also is the Executive Director of the City Heights Educational Plot—a cooperative arrangement with three San Diego schools, the San Diego Education Association, and San Diego State University focused on improving student achievement.

Caren Sax, Ed.D., teaches in the rehabilitation counseling graduate program and coordinates the certificate of rehabilitation technology with the College of Engineering and the Pupil Personnel Services credential with the Counseling and School Psychology Department at San Diego State University. Through federal- and state-funded grant projects, she also has directed research, demonstration, and training projects related to systems change efforts for school-to-adult life transition services for students with disabilities, the applications of assistive technology, and continuing education opportunities for community rehabilitation personnel.

Foreword

In Vivian Paley's (1992, Harvard University Press) book, *You Can't Say You Can't Play,* Paley, a kindergarten teacher, explores what it would be like to make inclusion the "rule" and exclusion "against the rules." With her kindergarten students, she proposes her new rule that "You can't say you can't play" and asks two questions of her students: "Is it fair?" and "Will it work?" She continues her exploration by visiting each of the upper-level grades in her school, telling the older students about her consideration of the rule for her younger students and asking their opinions. She repeats the same two questions to the older students: "Is it fair?" and "Will it work?"

Although the younger students generally agree that the rule is a good idea and embrace inclusion excitedly, the older students are more reluctant. They raise caveats, problems, and objections. One student says, "In your whole life you're not going to go through life never being excluded. So you may as well learn it now. Kids are going to get in the habit of thinking they're not going to be excluded so much and it isn't true" (Paley, 1992, p. 100). Another child offers a more hopeful perspective, "It would take a lot of getting used to, but it could happen. Right now there's a lot of saying no but if you kept at it a long time you could get it into your brain to say yes" (Paley, 1992, p. 99).

Inclusive Middle Schools raises the possibility that schools could "get it into" their systems to say "yes" to inclusion and "no" to exclusion. The authors (and their invited contributors) present a vision of what middle schools might look like if they were to take the principles of inclusion seriously, infusing a commitment to include all students into all aspects of curriculum, teaching, assessment, and school organization.

Just as the middle school students in Paley's book were cognizant that becoming inclusive would be hard, there is little illusion in this volume that the necessary changes will come quickly or easily. The levels of resistance to change are layered and powerful; doing things differently will take strong leadership and significant restructuring. For every example, as Kennedy and Fisher offer ideas about what inclusive middle schools could look like, we can ask ourselves: "What else would have to change for this to happen?" "If the curriculum is restructured to be multilevel and require active student participation, what will need to be rethought in terms of classroom management?" "If teachers are going to collaborate and co-plan lessons together, how will they find time for that collaboration, and where will they learn the skills needed to work together?" "If assessment is altered to reflect individual high standards for students, how will schools interface with larger accreditation and testing structures?"

Inclusive Middle Schools does not offer glib answers to such serious questions, but it does offer a vision of what is possible. Through powerful examples of classrooms in which teachers have altered their curriculum and teaching, we can begin to develop images of what could be and hope for what might be. Reading about these classrooms is exciting; many of them bear little or no resemblance to the middle schools we may now know or see, but it is not difficult to wish that the practices described here were commonplace.

It has been said that if we don't know where we're going, we'll surely end up somewhere else and that it's foolish to do the same things over and over again and expect different results. With those two principles in mind, Kennedy and Fisher have planted some powerful seeds of possibility and hope. There is little doubt that such change is necessary and that we cannot continue to teach adolescents in ways that alienate them from themselves and their communities. We will have to do things differently if we want our middle schools to nurture competent, caring young people who feel capable and empowered to change the world.

What is at stake here is not simply the future of middle schools but the future of our world. Middle schools function at an important pivotal point in students' education; students develop not only academic skills and competence but also a deep understanding of how the world works and their places in it. What do we want students to understand about diversity and how we respond to people who are different? What skills do we want them to have when faced with a peer who has cognitive or behavioral challenges? What inclination toward advocacy do we want them to have when they witness injustice or exclusion? A vision of a just and caring society must include our careful attention to not only *what* students are taught but *how* and in *what context*. Teaching students to be caring and empathic in settings that exclude some of their peers is an exercise is contradiction. We must model inclusion and compassion in all that we do; those will be the lessons students will observe and internalize.

We can return to Paley's two questions about her inclusion rule— "Is it fair?" and "Will it work?"—and ask them about inclusion in our middle schools. Is it fair to structure a high-quality education for all students, attentive to their individual needs but alert to the importance of maintaining a strong community? The answer is a clear yes.

Will it work? This book gives us hope that the answer is yes and details enough examples to ground that hope in reality. Let us not miss this opportunity to create the world we want for our students and with our students.

Mara Sapon-Shevin, Ed.D.
Professor of Inclusive Education
Syracuse University, New York

To Our Readers

THE WORK OF A MIDDLE SCHOOL

Adolescence: a word that can strike fear in the hearts of parents and professionals! Adolescence: a word that suggests first loves. Adolescence: a word that connotes identity crisis. Adolescence: a word that suggests physical change. Adolescence: a word that brings exciting new privileges. Adolescence: a word that means transition. Adolescence: a word that connotes terrible teens. Who are these members of our community who can elicit so many emotions? What school structures exist to socialize them into society? How are these individuals grouped?

These and other related questions were discussed when 18 strangers met in Costa Rica while sightseeing in the rainforest. The 1-day excursion lasted 12 hours and included riding the bus and eating, in addition to touring a jungle river, visiting the Poas volcano, and touring an oxcart factory. Five of the eighteen people were educators, and they began talking about their experiences with middle school students. These five included

1. Mr. Stroehlein, an upper school teacher from Germany
2. Dr. Washington, a university professor from California who trains middle school teachers
3. Mrs. Faye, a seventh- and eighth-grade English teacher at a private school in Texas
4. Ms. Greene, a district-level trainer on inclusion from London
5. Mr. Aguillar, a sixth-grade teacher from New York

When the 18 people introduced themselves at breakfast, they were surprised to learn that they had educational careers in common. They decided to sit together on the bus to the volcano, and they discussed issues that influence middle school students and schools. The conversation went something like this:

Mr. Stroehlein: In Germany, we separate kids when they are 10 years old. We know which ones are going to vocational schools and which ones are going to academic programs. I teach in the academic program, and our students perform well in school.

Ms. Greene:	Don't you have a difficult time with tracking? I mean, do you think you know what kids are capable of when they're 10 years old?
Mrs. Faye:	We know. Parents work hard to get their kids into our school. We test them, and they have to score well to be accepted. We also have very small class sizes. My English class had nine students last year, and that was my largest class.
Ms. Greene:	Shouldn't those opportunities be available to everyone?
Mr. Aguillar:	I know that they aren't available to students in my school. Our class sizes are three to four times larger than the average class size. Also, we have a lot of new teachers each year and few supplies for them to use in their classes.
Mr. Stroehlein:	I think about tracking a lot now. I'm not sure that the students in our vocational program couldn't do well in our academic program. If you don't track students, they all have a fair chance at a life and nothing is predetermined for them. Your students have more options when they graduate.
Mr. Aguillar:	I'm not sure that we don't track. Many schools say they don't track, but there is ability grouping within the classrooms. Schools also differ in their populations. My school is in an urban community and has a diverse student body. They have opportunities available to them that differ from those available to students in suburban schools. Rural schools also have challenges, such as course offerings, clubs, and student–teacher ratios. I think students get a different experience depending on where they go to school.

After the visit to the volcano, the conversation among the educators continued over lunch:

| Dr. Washington: | I want to return to the tracking and ability grouping conversation. Do you think it is possible for middle school students to be educated together? Do you think that achievement and belonging are attainable in inclusive schools? |

Ms. Greene:	Yes! We've been working on this in London for years. We have a lot of schools where good things are happening and students are doing great things.
Mr. Stroehlein:	I think it is a worthy goal. It sounds so American, though—you know, the land of opportunity. I'm not sure that it is possible where I live, but someday the preassigned roles will be challenged and people will think about other ways to conduct school.
Mrs. Faye:	There always will be parents who don't trust the public school system. I think our elite schools provide a needed alternative for families.
Mr. Aguillar:	Sure, it's possible. However, teachers need resources and skills to make it happen. We should structure schools to provide all students with the opportunity to succeed. We should also structure schools so that students and teachers are held to high expectations.

OVERVIEW OF INCLUSIVE MIDDLE SCHOOLS

It is possible to create middle schools that work for all students. It is possible to ensure that students achieve and belong. It is possible to teach without tracking. This book provides teachers, family members, and administrators with tools to accomplish these goals.

Chapter 1, co-written with Ian Pumpian, provides an overview of the need for inclusive middle schools. This chapter focuses on student achievement and includes a review of research on the topics of inclusion and school reform. It is clear that deficit models for thinking about student achievement must be challenged if inclusive education is to succeed.

Chapter 2 focuses on administrative issues that affect the quality of education that students receive in middle school. The chapter discusses how district and school policies can complement effective, inclusive educational practices in the classroom. Topics include school-based management, funding strategies, family involvement, positive school climates, and administrative leadership for inclusive education.

Chapter 3 addresses school teams that bring teachers together from across academic content areas to work with specific sets of students across the school year. This approach creates a cohort of students who interact with and are supported by a set of teachers who implement the students' daily classes and curriculum. Class scheduling also is discussed in this chapter. Traditional approaches to class scheduling have been based on brief exposures to isolated academic disciplines (e.g., math, social studies). However, such schedules create fragmented learning experiences for students. Strategies such as block scheduling allow middle schools to promote interdisciplinary learning that integrates core academic areas and provides students more time to complete assignments.

Chapter 4 discusses the middle school curriculum. Standards-based reform has had a significant influence on curriculum in general and on secondary school curriculum in particular. This chapter provides an overview of a process used to design inclusive curriculum units. In addition, specific strategies for creating accommodations and modifications to the curriculum are discussed.

Chapter 5 concentrates on instructional issues or the ways in which the curriculum is actually delivered to students. Differentiating instruction for mixed-ability groups is an important strategy in an inclusive middle school. This chapter outlines a variety of instructional strategies that teachers use to support various learning styles within the middle school classroom.

Chapter 6 considers assessment issues. Assessment information is used for a variety of purposes. Some assessments are used for accountability and are reported in the newspapers. Others are used by teachers to make instructional and curricular decisions.

Chapter 7, written by Caren Sax, highlights the use of instructional and assistive technology in inclusive middle school classrooms. In addition to the curriculum supports outlined in Chapters 4 and 5, students with disabilities need access to technology. The appropriate use of technology can result in changing roles for paraprofessionals, fewer curriculum accommodations or modifications, and increased independence for the student.

Chapter 8 illustrates the need for positive behavior support. Because challenging behavior can interfere with student success, educators are making use of positive behavior support. This approach, consistent with the Individuals with Disabilities Education Act (IDEA) Amendments of 1997 (PL 105-17), encompasses a functional assessment of why challenging behaviors occur, an interdisciplinary approach to problem solving, and the use of support strategies that promote gains in positive behavior.

Chapter 9, written by Nancy Frey, focuses on personal supports. Similar to the use of curriculum and technology supports, students need to gain access to personal supports, such as special education teachers, paraprofessionals, related services staff, and peers. This chapter provides an overview of the roles and responsibilities of general and special education teachers and how additional personal supports can be used in inclusive classrooms.

This book is a challenge to consider inclusive middle schools seriously and to make them a reality in the community. As Mr. Aguillar said at the end of the rainforest tour in Costa Rica, "We all have something to gain when students are successful."

Acknowledgments

This book represents our combined experiences in creating more effective middle school environments for students with and without disabilities. Our work in public schools has allowed us to learn a great deal since the 1990s regarding effective, doable, and meaningful approaches to supporting preadolescents as they emerge into adolescence and adulthood. This book is a summary of that learning process. However, because of the nature of this learning process, thanking all of those responsible for making this book a reality is not easy, nor, perhaps, even possible. Working as a team prevents anyone from truly "owning" an idea or innovation. We build on each other's ideas, brainstorm to increasingly more complex levels, and look to our colleagues for support and honest criticism.

We would like to acknowledge our editor at Paul H. Brookes Publishing Co., Lisa Benson, for believing in us and our ideas and thoughtfully moving us through the publication process (even when it was not easy). With her support, we were able to closely work with and learn from teachers, administrators, and students. Being able to step back and chronicle years of change often is difficult to keep in perspective. The teachers who contributed to this book are phenomenal role models, teacher-leaders, and catalysts for change in their schools. They, along with their colleagues, have pushed the boundaries for creating more inclusive schools. And, of course, we must thank all of the students who keep us grounded in what works and what needs to be changed in classrooms.

Some of the early work for this book came from federally funded grants—the Consortium on Inclusive Schooling Practices, No. H086V4007 (to Douglas Fisher), and Social Inclusion Research Project, No. H086D40009 (to Craig H. Kennedy). Prior versions of parts of this book were first developed through these projects with the assistance of Virginia Roach, Cheryl Jorgensen, Anne Smith, Gloria Kishi, Tiina Itkonen, Lisa Sharon Cushing, Jacqui Farmer-Kearns, Ian Pumpian, Gail McGregor, and Chris Salisbury. We are grateful for their time, support of, and thoughts about inclusive education for all students.

We also would like to thank each of our contributors who offered insightful perspectives that added greater breadth and depth to the book. Each has his or her own unique manner of examining an issue, analyzing its impact, and eloquently summarizing next steps. They have contributed greatly to this book.

We would like to give special thanks to Mara Sapon-Shevin, who wrote the foreword to this book from her unique position as a social justice advocate. She sees the world as it can be, and we appreciate her support for our work.

Finally, we would like to thank our families and friends for their patience and support during the deadlines, hours of writing, and agonizing over details. We are extremely fortunate to have such caring people in our lives.

To the memory of Thomas G. Haring (CHK)

*To the students and their families who have shared
their stories, struggles, and successes (DF)*

Inclusive Middle Schools

"Human life always involves a continuous dialogue between the actual and the possible." —*François Jacob*

1

Parallels Between the Problems and Possibilities in Contemporary Education

Ian Pumpian

Douglas Fisher

Craig H. Kennedy

> *Inclusion is a part of the very culture of a school or school district and defines how students, teachers, administrators and others view the potential of children. Hence, inclusion has implications for how schools are organized and restructured, the curriculum, instruction, teacher training, and the types of materials and instructional technology used in the school. In fact, many schools have become inclusive schools when they restructured under current school reform efforts. (Roach, 1995, p. 7)*

The underlying value behind inclusive education is that all children should be welcomed members of the school, classroom, and larger community. A great deal of research has been done on supporting individual students with disabilities in general education classes (Brown et al., 1989; Cushing & Kennedy, 1997; Kleinert, Kearns, & Kennedy, 1997; Ryndak & Alper, 1996; Sax, Fisher, & Pumpian, 1996). The resulting substantial database indicates that it is more than possible to provide students with disabilities access to the best available educational practice and to demonstrate positive student achievement in inclusive settings (Fisher, 1996; Helmstetter, Peck, & Giangreco, 1994; Kennedy, Shukla, & Fryxell, 1997).

Unfortunately, most service delivery models have failed to make effective and inclusive practices readily available and accessible to students with disabilities (Danielson & Bellamy, 1989; U.S. Department of Education, 1996). After almost 20 years of specific federal support through the Individuals with Disabilities Education Act (IDEA) of 1990, PL 101-476, (first through the Education for All Handicapped Children Act of 1975 [PL 94-142]), fewer than half of the students who receive special education services graduate with a diploma (U.S. Department of Education, 1993). According to the National Longitudinal Transition Study, only 20% of students with disabilities are independent in the domains of work, residential activities, and social activities 3–5 years after completing high school (Wagner, 1993).

Increasingly, schools are being held accountable not only for the achievement of students with disabilities but also for the achievement of students without disabilities. Data on student achievement underscore the evidence of the school district's failure to make best and emerging educational practices available to all students (Meier, 1995; Sautter, 1994). This impact is most significant in larger communities (U.S. Department of Education, 1996). For example, more than 40% of students in urban districts drop out and more than 70% read, write, and compute below grade level (Espinosa & Ochoa, 1992).

The fact is that student achievement among all students needs to become a national priority. Focusing on the achievement of all students is logical and justified because many students with disabilities also are socioeconomically, culturally, and linguistically diverse (Atkins, 1994). Hence, education reform is important but only if it is designed and evaluated in terms of its impact on student achievement.

A great deal is known about policies and practices that are positively linked to student achievement, particularly for students with disabilities in inclusive settings. The literature substantiates, for example, the importance of active parent–school partnerships (Buswell & Schaffner, 1995); challenging and relevant curricula (Fisher, Sax, & Jorgensen, 1998); individualized supports and accommodations (Ryndak & Alper, 1996); positive behavior support and strategies (Lovett, 1996; Sprague, Sugai, & Walker, 1998); peer interactions (Cushing & Kennedy, 1997); transition planning (Certo, Pumpian, Fisher, Storey, & Smalley, 1997); and access to the full range of programs and supports available to children without disabilities (Meyer, Park, Grenot-Scheyer, Schwartz, & Harry, 1998).

Tremendous parallels exist between the problems and solutions in educational reform and the problems and solutions in promoting effective inclusive education. Because a high percentage of students with disabilities are educated in urban settings, these problems and solutions overlap and cannot be viewed separately; unfortunately, they are. Specific reform initiatives, and those involved in implementing these reforms, are fragmented within and across site, district, state, and national levels. Reform is essential, but only as a *means to an end.* Reform usually implies a set of strategies designed to make change, but to what end? The educator's work must first and foremost be about *improving student achievement.*

To many people, the problems and needs of America seem insurmountable. It is easy to conjure up images of massive poverty, dilapidated private and public structures, crime, vandalism, alcohol and other drug problems, child abuse and neglect, and gang fights (Atkins, 1994). Urban and suburban housing and employment patterns continue to result in ethnic and racial segregation and unemployment. African American urban males are more likely to die from a gunshot wound than from any other cause (Atkins, 1994). For many, these urban realities become correlated with the fact that more than 75% of urban students are from ethnic minorities and speak more than 150 languages. More than 15% of urban children are still learning English language skills, and an enormous disparity exists in the educational achievement curves of these students. *To people who presume causal relationships in these correlations, educational reform appears pointless.* People who feel defeated by the system often seek to escape confronting the problem altogether (e.g., moving to suburban areas, voting for private school voucher initiatives).

Other people, however, are careful to look for ways to tap into the strength and resilience in these educational settings. They know that children cannot be held accountable for their educational failure when little public equity exists, especially when factors such as the size, age, condition, and resources of school buildings; the amount of per-student spending; and the degree of tracking all are negatively represented in the inner cities. That urban children show no marked differences from others when they enter school and progressively fail in comparison after each year of attendance (Sautter, 1994) turns the attention to school and community structures (e.g., policies and practices) and away from a pessimistic deficit view of children and the expectations held for them.

Some people do believe educational reform is possible. Often, they demonstrate that change is possible by getting involved in building new schools with widespread community partnerships or by aggressively challenging traditional tracking, testing, curriculum, or pedagogy. The reforms that are most successful in these settings seem to have a grass roots means of engaging and empowering parents and members of the community to partner with the administrators, teachers, and students of the school.

To many, the accompanying problems and needs of children with disabilities, especially those with severe disabilities, seem insurmountable. Adaptive devices and equipment (e.g., gastrointestinal tubes), seizures, drooling, behavioral disruptions, and unusual verbalizations are outside the realm of experience and understanding of many people. These realities associated with disabilities become correlated with the fact that educating children with disabilities is expensive and challenging. Special education and inclusion appear to be pointless and counterproductive to those who conclude that disability is the cause of poor educational achievement. People who draw such conclusions question how teachers' time and resources can be spent on these children at the expense of "normal kids who could really learn something." Historically, when students with disabilities failed educationally, they were pitied, and then society attempted to distance itself from them and their families and their educational needs (Trent, 1994).

Other people, however, are careful to look for ways of tapping into the strength and resilience of these children and their families. They know that children can hardly be held accountable for their educational failure, because with effective services and supports, all children, even those with severe disabilities, can function and contribute across a wide range of education, employment, home, and social endeavors. The failure to establish effective service delivery models and implement effective and emerging best practices is a public decision that becomes blurred when children are pitied and their parents and advocates are devalued.

People who believe that inclusive education is possible work hard to bring resources to ideas, ideas to actions, and actions to outcomes. Their reforms seem to be most successful in settings in which administrative leadership is supportive of inclusion, general and special educators are partners in curriculum design and instruction, and parents and other community members are involved and empowered in the life of the school. These reforms seem to be most pervasive and sustained when special education reform and the inclusion of students with disabilities is solidly based in general education. General education reform efforts need to be at all levels of educational policy and practice.

Aligning education reform to improve the achievement of all students requires attention to philosophical and structural needs. The remainder of this chapter is organized by a series of discussions and recommendations related to a proposed set of reform challenges. These challenges are presented to illustrate the similarities between issues that confront contemporary education and those confronted by students with disabilities. The reforms and challenges presented here include

- Challenging the current societal stereotypes for explaining student achievement
- Identifying and positively altering the public education structural variables that strongly correlate with student achievement
- Utilizing a process for connecting and influencing policy based on implementation experiences at the building and classroom level
- Establishing district commitment to inclusive education reform at the administrative level

CHALLENGING THE CURRENT SOCIETAL STEREOTYPES FOR EXPLAINING STUDENT ACHIEVEMENT

The educational achievements of students continue to be discouraging, especially among ethnically diverse and low-income learners (Espinosa & Ochoa, 1992). Similarly, educational outcomes for youth with disabilities are dismal (Fisher, 1996; Wagner, 1993). Espinosa and Ochoa (1992) documented a 6-year longitudinal study of the educational achievement of and the school resources available to ethnically diverse and low-income students within the context of state and national education reform initiatives. Their study revealed the inadequacy of the deficit model for explaining poor school achievement among certain groups. Similarly, special educators have been scrutinizing and abandoning a deficit model that has long influenced special education approaches and philosophy (Skrtic, 1995). Nonetheless, Sautter (1994) concluded that the deficit model has dominated education. His review suggested that environmental issues eventually become viewed as student deficits. Eventually, as educators, policymakers, and the public attempt to overcome these deficits, they establish negative stereotypes of, and discrimination toward, students (Atkins, 1994). Nieto (1996) argued that racism, other forms of discrimination, and limited expectations of student abilities have a direct impact on achievement. She proposed that these practices are pervasive and lead to categorizing people on the basis of obvious and subtle traits. From these categories, fixed expectations are developed. Most important, potential is presumed; and resources, policies, and practices, both material and psychological, are metered accordingly. With less support, student achievement is diminished and a self-fulfilling prophecy is created.

Similarly, researchers have challenged expectations and attitudes commonly associated with disability and severity of disability. Contemporary special education policy and practice are derived from a litigious history, which established the obvious link between ineducability *and* the failure to provide education (*Pennsylvania Association for Retarded Citizens v. Commonwealth of Pennsylvania*, 1971).

A need exists to challenge and test the adequacy of the commonly accepted conceptualization for explaining student achievement, a perspective that limits reforms and continues to dominate educational research, analysis, and policy (Fraser, 1995). Similarities in traditional approaches to explaining student achievement are found across general and special education (Herrnstein & Murray, 1994; Skrtic, 1995). There is a need to coordinate these common yet parallel efforts to effectively launch a long-term shift in educational policy that affects all students and all concerned stakeholders (Sautter, 1994).

Historically, deficit models were derived from those who assumed limited potential to be characteristic of certain races, who assumed laziness and lack of ambition of certain cultures, and who assumed lack of ability and normalcy to be characteristic of particular disability labels (Herrnstein & Murray, 1994; Skrtic, 1995). These models and assumptions have supported policies that have had a negative impact on students of low socioeconomic status and students of all ethnic and racial identities, as well as on individuals with disabilities (Lytle, 1992; Sowell, 1994; Wolfe, 1995).

The public discourse within which educational theory, research, policy, and practice are shaped also assumes a public commitment to standards of equity, fairness, and reasonableness derived from constitutional law, as well as from federal, state, and local statutes. A long line of judicial demands for equity, fairness, and reasonableness, from *Brown v. Board of Education* (1954), to *Lau v. Nichols* (1974) to *Pennsylvania Association for Retarded Citizens v. Commonwealth of Pennsylvania* (1971), supports the spirit and intent of such statutes. They demonstrate the danger of assuming that the equity, fairness, and reasonableness sought will always adequately inform policy and change practice. When such assumptions are embedded in research, it appears logical to adopt a deficit model and to seek the source of perceived problems within the person or group that shows symptoms (Pool & Page, 1995; Sleeter, 1996). Such assumptions, coupled with a deficit model, may encourage a lack of awareness of the nature or extent of social problems (Atkins, 1994). For example, do state assessment programs conceal disparities and inequities? And are these results linked to discriminatory attitudes and practices that negatively affect the state's lowest achievers: urban students, African Americans, Caucasians of low socioeconomic status,

Native Americans, Latinos, Asian Americans, and most assuredly those with disabilities?

The failure and unwillingness to disaggregate data result in state and district educational achievement curves that conceal enormous disparities among student populations. Espinosa and Ochoa (1992) found structural variables that correlate strongly with schools' student achievement averages and with unequal distribution of educational resources. These findings suggest the need to abandon commonly held assumptions and instead adopt a philosophy that views educational achievement and underachievement as flowing from structural and pedagogical conditions (Martusewicz & Reynolds, 1994). Their findings led Espinosa and Ochoa to propose a public equity model through which discourse can move from blaming people for their condition to examining the conditions faced by schools from a macro perspective and, for the first time, permitting all schools to provide equitable and sufficient educational services regardless of students' economic, ethnic, racial, cultural, linguistic, or ability characteristics.

In summary, the historical persistence and adherence to a deficit model has had detrimental effects for both general and special education. Neither system has benefited from this approach. This model has fostered a tendency to blame the victim when students in the most challenging environments do not succeed in school. It reinforces a pity-the-victim mentality when evaluating poor educational achievements for students with disabilities, especially those with severe disabilities. Whether the victim is blamed or pitied, scrutiny is diverted from the roles and responsibilities of schools to promote educational achievement (Feinberg & Soltis, 1992; Nieto, 1996; Pulliam & Van Patten, 1995).

Similarly, researchers and others concerned with special education have attempted to diminish the powerful, persistent, and negative effects of the deficit model by demonstrating how full, rich, positive, and typical the lives and accomplishments of people with disabilities can be (Biklen, 1992; Shapiro, 1993). Nowhere have these demonstrations been more pronounced than among individuals who manifest the most obvious and severe physical, behavioral, and cognitive challenges (Brown et al., 1983; Brown et al., 1991). These demonstrations challenge hundreds of years of stereotypes, proving that people with severe disabilities can attend school with, and learn effectively alongside, their typically developing peers (Fisher, Sax, Pumpian, Rodifer, & Kreikemeirer, 1997; National Association of State Boards of Education [NASBE], 1992; Ryndak & Alper, 1996), recreate and socialize with a broad circle of friends and acquaintances (Kennedy, Horner, & Newton, 1989), live in typical homes and apartments within their community with typically developing roommates and family members (O'Brien, 1994), and work in meaningful private and public sector jobs (Pumpian, Fisher, Certo, & Smalley, 1997). However, the savage inequalities and the undereducation and achievement of students in special education remain pervasive (Wagner, 1993). There is a need to unify attempts to establish more accurate, positive, and constructive views of all students and use existing and emerging information derived from education reforms, research, and practice to improve schools and schooling.

IDENTIFYING AND POSITIVELY ALTERING THE PUBLIC EDUCATION STRUCTURAL VARIABLES THAT CORRELATE STRONGLY WITH STUDENT ACHIEVEMENT

The deficit model has reinforced discrimination against and created limited expectations for students from low-income families, African American students, and students with disabilities (i.e., all minority students). The effects are fully connected with fundamental school structures. These structures, in turn, are established and maintained in educational policy and practice (Delpit, 1995; Pulliam & Van Patten, 1995).

> *Each of these structural options has an underlying philosophy and approach with important implications for the academic achievement and failure of students. Existing societal inequities, the structure of the schools, and the culture of students and communities must be understood in tandem. Children of different backgrounds are educated differently by our schools, and the differences children bring to school have a profound effect on what they gain from their educational experiences. (Nieto, 1996, p. 33)*

Nieto (1996) argued that it is difficult to separate what is discriminatory from what is structural. Her arguments and research are most poignant and critical with regard to tracking and ability grouping. Oakes (1985, 1992) reported that tracking has had a negative impact on achievement; integration; innovative pedagogy; student and teacher expectations; and lifelong attitudes about schools, school experiences, and the future. Goodlad (1984) drew similar conclusions regarding ability grouping. Nonetheless, tracking and ability groups are pervasive and affect large numbers of ethnically and linguistically diverse children (Oakes, 1992; Pool & Page, 1995). As a result, the very policies and practices most likely to have a negative impact on students' educational achievement are ironically most common in the schools that these students attend (Espinosa & Ochoa, 1992; Nieto, 1996).

Similarly, the maintenance, justification, and proliferation of special day classes and segregated special education schools are a major source of debate and controversy (Fuchs & Fuchs, 1995). Undeniably, this is the most obvious, accepted, and institutionalized example of tracking and ability grouping in schools today (Fisher, 1996; NASBE, 1992). Compelling arguments and evidence critique such placements (Sax et al., 1996; Taylor, 1988), demonstrate effective inclusive options (Ford, Davern, & Schnorr, 1991; Ryndak & Alper, 1996), and provide a legal bias of and basis for integration (Roach & Caruso, 1997). However, proponents for a full continuum of placement options tend to cite data that suggest that typical classrooms and teachers do not have the skills, attitudes, or resources to meet the diverse needs of most students in special education (Fuchs & Fuchs, 1995; Shanker, 1995). These researchers and policymakers tend to advocate as much for maintaining and believing in a separate education system as they would for reforms that might improve skills or attitudes within general education and strategies to integrate and merge special and general education (Pugach, 1995; Zigmond & Baker, 1995). There is a need to unify educators and others who see the similarity in the structural practices of and limitations in tracking, ability grouping, and traditional special education placement practices. There is a need to unify reformers who are calling for and attempting to detrack our schools (Hill, 1995; Wheelock, 1992) with the parallel effort of special educators and others who are promoting and emphasizing a need for a continuum of *special services* and supports rather than a continuum of *special placements* (Fisher, Sax, & Pumpian, 1996). There is a need to unify policymakers, practitioners, parents, and others who believe that educational reform and achievement is directly related to dismantling structures that unnecessarily segregate children from each other and the best of what schooling can offer (Brown et al., 1989; Roach, 1991).

The relationship between ability grouping and pedagogy also must be recognized. Nieto wrote,

> Students in the lowest levels, for example, are most subjected to rote memorization and worn methods, as their teachers often feel that these are the children who need, first, to master the basics. Until the basics are learned, the thinking goes, creative methods are a frill that these students can ill afford. Poor children and those most alienated by the schools are once again the losers. The cycle of school failure is repeated: the students most in need are placed in the lowest-level classes and exposed to the drudgery of drill and repetition; school becomes more boring and senseless everyday and the students become discouraged and drop out. (1996, p. 89)

The unilateral concentration on basic skill instruction also receives support from many special education researchers whose methodology and
statistical measures are most sensitive to improvement in isolated basic
skills performance (Lerner, 1993; Olsen, 1994). Other research method-
ologies that are more sensitive to longitudinal changes in performance
and attitude are needed.

Given the link between tracking (including grouping and special
day classes) and other school policies and practices, simply detracking
and desegregating schools will not be effective. Instead, there is a need
to combine detracking and desegregation with other major structural
changes associated with student achievement, such as cooperative learning, peer tutoring, multilevel instruction, multicultural curriculum, full-
service schools, interdisciplinary curriculum and teaching, parent and
community involvement, social marketing and policy issues of finance,
governance, professional development, curriculum, assessment, and
accountability (Andreasen, 1995; Brooks & Brooks, 1993; Jacobs, 1989;
NASBE, 1996; Sleeter, 1996; Tomlinson, 1995).

Berends and King (1994) suggested that these structures, and related reforms, might be organized under four general categories: student experience, professional life of teachers, governance, and parent
and community involvement. Further, they found little evidence of any
systemic initiatives that truly coordinated reforms across these broad
and overlapping categories. There is a need for structural change coupled with detracking. Table 1.1 expands Nieto's basic structural analysis.

There is a need to aggressively incorporate career development,
employment opportunities, mentoring, apprenticeships, and wages into
the educational experience of youth (Kyle, 1995). Further, there is a need
to ensure that this examination and altering of schools is framed within
a model of building public equity (Espinosa & Ochoa, 1992; Poplin &
Weeres, 1992). Plans and actions must reflect the values and participation of all education stakeholders. Many of these stakeholders have
heretofore either been minimized (by their exclusion from reform) or
isolated (by their parallel attempts at reform).

UTILIZING A PROCESS FOR CONNECTING AND INFLUENCING POLICY BASED ON IMPLEMENTATION EXPERIENCES AT THE BUILDING AND CLASSROOM LEVEL

Despite the extensive literature on policy development, social scientists
have offered relatively little advice on how to anticipate and avoid policy implementation difficulties (Fuhrman, 1993). Historically, policy

Table 1.1. Structural variables to change

Testing	As the basis for segregating and sorting students physically and by teacher expectations (Figueroa & Garcia, 1994)
Curriculum	As the source of boredom and disengagement (Poplin & Weeres, 1992); as racist and classist notions of ability
Pedagogy	Unmotivating instruction that relies solely and mechanistically on textbooks and chalk and talk methods (Goodlad, 1984); reflects the unsubstantiated belief in the pedagogy of poverty (Haberman, 1991)
Employability	Untenable outcomes of existing unemployment, particularly among ethnically diverse youth and youth with disabilities, not structurally considered as an educational need; many urban students and those with disabilities drop out of school when need or opportunity for wage earning pre sents itself (Lichtenstein, 1993)
Physical structure	Ill-equipped, dilapidated buildings, uninviting and fortress-like (Espinosa & Ochoa, 1992; Kozol, 1991); provides a stark contrast to goals of teaching and learning (Nieto, 1996) despite existence of innovative building designs and technology-enhanced, full-service school sites that provide educational, health, and social benefits (Dryfoos, 1994)
Roles of students, teachers, parents, community	Devalued, uninvolved, disempowered, alienated, and discouraged; window-dressing involvement in the governance structures of schools and educational policy making (U.S. Department of Education, 1994); ample demonstrations and evidence indicate that schools founded on participation, community partnerships, critical theory (Espinosa & Ochoa, 1992), democratic schooling (Apple & Beane, 1995), shared decision making (Bonstignl, 1992), and leadership (Sergiovanni, 1992) have significant strategic educational, financial, and social advantages and promise over those that are not (Fullan, 1993; Fullan & Hargreaves, 1996; Sizer, 1992)

development has been divorced from practice, and policymakers have been unable to anticipate problems that are likely to be encountered during the implementation of policies that have already been formulated (Baer, 1993; Lieberman, 1995). Parenthetically, much research is divorced from practice as well, resulting in an analogous set of researched strategies too decontextualized to be replicated in a top-down ordered sequence by the research (Wang, 1997).

Given the fractured nature of many districts and their bureaucratic culture, it is essential to closely link policy implementation to practice. It is the absence of this link that creates a highly fractured environment. New programs and model projects often have little or conflicting policy support. *Backward mapping* provides the methodological links necessary to support positive integration of school reform and inclusion. In general, backward mapping begins with the desired outcomes, determines the most direct ways of producing those outcomes, and then maps actions backward (effects to causes) through the organizational hierarchy to the highest-level policy that must be developed to realize the desired outcome (Weiner & Vining, 1992). Clearly, backward mapping is not a top-down approach but rather a bidirectional method and requires significant involvement of many stakeholders (Carlson, 1996).

The process of backward mapping has been explored in great depth by Elmore (1980), who concluded that if policies do not make sense for practitioners at the grass roots, implementation, and delivery levels, the likelihood is that they are not going to be meaningful for policymakers at the top level of the system. The problem-solving approach implied by backward mapping forces an analytical framework on discussions that relate to program implementation and delivery within the context of the outcomes to be achieved (Elmore, 1980).

The approach is particularly useful in two ways. First, the process of backward mapping is valuable in meeting the need to research and analyze *successful policy strategies* for implementing effective inclusive educational reforms in schools and classrooms. *It enables policymakers to have a greater understanding of where to focus resources* (human, financial, technical, and knowledge based) that are needed for overcoming problems rather than assume *a priori* that they fully understand how to solve the problems. In this approach, the most concrete sets of activities and behaviors are examined from the site implementation team to the policy level in which priorities can be established and concrete steps taken to bring resources to where they are most needed. Second, the process of backward mapping meets the need to assist, support, and coordinate the implementation across site and district teams because it provides critical information and pertinent insights about what works and why and, conversely, what does not work and why. Hence, this interactive process affects and benefits all stakeholders by creating a responsive means to identify actual stumbling blocks that tend to inhibit improved results for all students, as well as authentic building blocks that enhance such results.

ESTABLISHING DISTRICT
COMMITMENT TO INCLUSIVE EDUCATION
REFORM AT THE ADMINISTRATIVE LEVEL

Approaching inclusive education reform in a district through the office of the Director of Special Education is *necessary but not sufficient*. The Director of Special Education is in the middle of a multilayered bureaucracy, often removed from the top policymakers *and* classroom practice. Without an approach that establishes buy-in from top policymakers and empowers the Director of Special Education, as well as an approach that connects the director's office to a site-based consumer- and practitioner-centered process, the goals of inclusive education reform will be underrealized. It has been argued that such shortcomings have been perpetuated by funded special education projects that depend almost unilaterally on the Director of Special Education. Major initiatives, public attention, and system influences are announced by the superintendent, not assistant or area superintendents or program directors. These initiatives are endorsed by the school board; coordinated within the bargaining agreement; and communicated to area and assistant superintendents, teachers, and parents.

Therefore, there is a need to connect the district's special education department and leadership with the district's overall leadership and reform agenda. Directors need to be empowered, and new approaches and entry points are necessary. There also is a need for a project that connects an inclusive reform agenda with school sites that are actually engaged in planning, implementing, and integrating site-based reforms with emerging best inclusive schooling practices. The use of district and site action research teams connected by way of a backward mapping process is needed in this regard. Directors must influence their superintendents to consider the impact of their reform initiatives on all students. However, the superintendent, and not the Director of Special Education, must be the primary policy spokesperson for the district.

Tremendous parallels exist between the needs for reform in general education and the needs in special education. Together, general and special educators can address historically limiting stereotypes and create service delivery systems that are culturally responsive and simultaneously address student achievement. This book focuses on schools in which students achieve and belong, schools that provide a range of supports and services in the general education classroom for all students, and schools that are structured to ensure success.

I

SCHOOL STRUCTURES

"Human well-being is not based merely on individual characteristics, but is a result of the individual's relation to other people."
—Simo Vehmas

2

Administrative Leadership

Craig H. Kennedy

Consider the basic aspects of a student's school day—which school he or she attends, in which classroom he or she is placed, who is assigned to be his or her teacher(s), which classes he or she attends with, which students he or she interacts, and which types of additional supports he or she might receive. Each of these aspects is based on decisions made by educational administrators at the district and school levels. Although the individualized education program (IEP) team makes decisions about supporting a student with disabilities, administrative leaders set the context for what a student (with or without disabilities) is likely, or un-likely, to receive within a school system.

The decisions made by educational administrators are often broad and policy oriented, and their effects are not immediately observable. However, those decisions lay the foundations for what teachers can ex-pect to accomplish within their classrooms. Sometimes, these decisions are detrimental; for example, when a principal decides to establish *school teams* based on grade level (see Chapter 3), except for special educators who form their own teams, general and special education teachers are discouraged from collaborating with each other. Having special and general educators on separate teams causes problems in identifying meeting times, finding opportunities to plan for curriculum integration and adaptation, and excluding students with disabilities from being part of school team decision making.

A less visible but important administrative decision is the development of *neighborhood schools* within a school district. The concept of neighborhood schools is based on students with and without disabilities attending their local neighborhood school (Sailor, 1991). In school districts that opt to place students in neighborhood schools, students with disabilities attend the same school as their peers. Benefits of this arrangement include greater school and community commitment to inclusive educational practices, equalizing the presence of individual differences across schools within a district, facilitating social relationships across school and home among students, continuity in transitions from one school to the next, and a realization on the part of school personnel that students cannot be denied access to the school based on individual characteristics (e.g., a particular sensory or physical disability) (Sailor, in press).

Conversely, if administrators opt to arrange for school placements on the basis of exemption, then students may be placed in schools that specialize in a particular student characteristic (e.g., type of disability). Although this approach can have a beneficial effect in some situations (e.g., magnet schools for all students with musical talents), it has traditionally been linked with practices that exclude students with disabilities. School districts that have a history of placement based on student exemptions often have schools designated for particular types of disabilities. For example, in some school districts, particular schools are designated for students with behavior disorders or severe disabilities. These cluster schools draw students with a particular disability from the school district to a single school, creating a high presence of one type of disability in a setting. Historically, the notion of student exemptions has led school districts to contract with schools outside their system to educate a particular group of students (e.g., those with multiple disabilities). As a result, individual communities and schools do not feel responsible for educating a diverse student population but only for educating those students who meet the nonexemption criteria—a perspective that is philosophically antithetical to inclusive practices, as well as a pragmatic barrier.

Even when administrative policies are not obvious to teachers, families, or community members, they still affect teachers' practices and the education that students receive. Because administrative policies have an impact on the quality of a student's education, it seems appropriate to devote a chapter to how district- and school-level administrators can have a positive impact on schools that are becoming more inclusive. Although administrative policies on their own cannot create inclusive learning environments, the types of policies enacted in a district or school can have a profound enabling effect on the ability of a school, its teachers, and its community members to create more inclusive learning environments.

LAYERS OF EDUCATIONAL POLICY

The preceding section illustrates how local administrative decisions can affect school function. However, local decisions are embedded in a web of policies enacted at the state and federal levels. This policy structure has a hierarchical arrangement in which state education agency (SEA) policies overrule local education agency (LEA) policies, and federal policies overrule SEA policies, unless otherwise specified by law. This means that the enactment of policies at the federal level has a trickle-down effect through SEAs and LEAs to individual schools and teachers.

At its broadest level, American educational policies are defined at the federal level. Examples of federal policies include the Individuals with Disabilities Education Act (IDEA) Amendments of 1997 (PL 105-17), the Americans with Disabilities Act (ADA) of 1990 (PL 101-336), and Goals 2000: Educate America Act of 1994 (PL 103-227). These efforts by national policymakers help induce positive changes at the state and local levels with a degree of continuity across states. Such initiatives are based on concerns voiced at a national level that certain practices or conditions in individual states are undesirable or inadequate. The goal of federal initiatives is to improve services or standards evenly across the various regions of the United States. For example, prior to the implementation of the Education for All Handicapped Children Act of 1975 (PL 94-142) states and school districts decided whether public schools should provide educational opportunities to students with disabilities. The net result was a range of local practices that resulted in students with disabilities being excluded from public schools or being educated in separate schools designed specifically for students with disabilities (Trent, 1994). Following the adoption of IDEA '97, all SEAs and LEAs were required to provide a public school education for *all* students with disabilities. The law included a set of provisions to help ensure that appropriate services were provided to students and their families (e.g., meeting the requirements of placing each student in the least restrictive environment).

Federal initiatives, such as the Education for All Handicapped Children Act of 1975, have had an impact on the types and quality of services that are accessible to people with disabilities. When a law such as the Education for All Handicapped Children Act of 1975 is implemented, it requires that SEAs implement policies that are consistent with the federal law but allows SEAs to tailor how they meet those mandates to the needs of each state. For example, in some states the implementation of the Education for All Handicapped Children Act of 1975 was associated with statewide efforts to eliminate segregated services designed only for people with disabilities. States that initiated their own proactive policies in light of the Education for All Handicapped Children Act of 1975, such as Oregon and Minnesota, often exceeded the minimum standards for practices outlined in the federal law. Such state-level efforts have resulted in innovations that have evolved into supported employment, supported living, and inclusive education. Such practices have emerged at the local and state levels, at least in part, because of federal initiatives that emphasize the importance of inclusion for people with and without disabilities.

Once states interpret federal initiatives and launch their own initiatives, it is the responsibility of local entities to implement policies and practices to achieve the federal and SEA initiatives. It is at the local level that innovative practices that lead to improved student outcomes are developed, implemented, and tested by LEAs and schools (Baer, 1993). Although federal and state initiatives can specify a framework for how educational services can be provided to students, the details of how those goals should be achieved is the responsibility of LEAs, schools, and teachers. This intersection between federal and state policy and how schools and teachers educate students with and without disabilities is the basis for what is described as *best practices*.

The term *best practices* is used by educators to encapsulate current research-based knowledge about the most effective strategies for achieving valued educational goals. Best practices, by their nature, are continuously evolving, being tested, and being debated by professionals involved in educational endeavors. Because public education is mandated in the United States for all students, federal and SEA initiatives have been the source for new and innovative educational practices. However, it is the daily contact with students that innovative educational practices affect.

HOW EDUCATIONAL
ADMINISTRATORS SUPPORT BEST PRACTICES

Where do LEA administrators (e.g., school district superintendents, special education directors) and school administrators (e.g., principals, vice principals) fit into the mix of policies and practices? Their role as administrators is *central* to the adoption of best practices by teachers (Janus, 1994). In many respects, LEA and school administrators are gatekeepers, allowing the individuals whom they directly or indirectly supervise to innovate and work toward improving existing educational practices. An important role of LEA and school administrators is to assess current and future educational policies and to take steps to prepare schools and teachers to meet these changes successfully.

In proactively supporting best practices, educational administrators can enable and facilitate schools and teachers to adopt, and even develop, innovative practices from which students and others will benefit. Educational administrators can help schools and teachers to innovate by 1) suggesting directions for improving educational practices, 2) allowing grass roots innovation among teachers and community members, and 3) providing leadership that creates an environment supportive of improvement and new initiatives.

Discussions on reforming educational practices have focused on issues of school leadership (Murphy & Louis, 1999). This focus is based on the observation that federal and SEA policy changes are filtered through LEAs and *enacted* by administrators at each school in an LEA. This places school leaders in the role of creating school environments that are receptive and making shifts in pedagogical practices based on larger policy changes. Creating schools that can adapt positively to change requires active leadership on the part of school administrators. It has been cited by researchers in educational leadership that if a competent and innovative principal can be found, then a competent and innovative school will be found (Klecker & Loadman, 1999). This suggests the important role that school leadership plays in fostering improvements in educational practices. Interestingly, recent developments in how school administrators can create more effective schools focus on leadership changes that place the school administration in a secondary rather than a primary role in creating educational innovation. This observation suggests the enabling and facilitative roles that school administrators can play.

The following sections outline a set of practices in which school administrators engage and that have been associated with improvements in school functioning and creating more inclusive learning environments.

MISSION AND VISION

How a school defines its purpose and how it pursues its goals is associated with the outcomes it achieves (Gilbert, 1981–1982). This is at the heart of efforts to assist schools in defining their mission and vision. The goal of defining a school's mission and vision is to enable the school to find its focus through the dialogue of individuals.

Mission is the overarching set of goals that a school tries to achieve. For example, a school might set as its mission to improve the social and academic success of all students. In general, mission statements focus on a primary set of objectives contributed by people in the school. *Vision* is the perspective of how to achieve a school's mission. For example, a school that is interested in facilitating inclusive practices might define its vision as bringing together educational and community leadership to make a difference in children's lives. Together, a school's mission and vision help define for people inside and outside the school what the organization values and focuses on in its daily activities (Lipman, 1997).

A school that defines its mission as creating the engineers of the future will have a different perspective on what the role of the school is compared with a school that defines its mission as improving the social and academic success for all students. One should note, however, that although these two mission statements are different, they are not incompatible. The importance of mission and values statements is that people work together to define what it is they value and strive to achieve.

There are two aspects of creating a school's mission and vision. First, it is a process that brings together all of the people who contribute to a school (e.g., students, families, community members) to define the school's purpose. Second, it provides a concrete set of statements about what these individuals are working toward creating. When done effectively, the creation of a school's mission and vision statement allows for the articulation of what all members of a school community should be working to achieve and provides a unifying theme around which to coordinate activities.

SCHOOL/COMMUNITY-BASED MANAGEMENT

Schools are part of the communities in which they exist. However, only since the 1980s have educators realized the importance of this observation (Talley & Schrag, 1999). Traditionally, schools have been thought of as bastions separate from their communities. They were places where people congregated from various areas to educate children and then left at the end of the day. Unfortunately, this type of view, which has its roots in a higher education approach to middle school education (see Chapter 3), creates a strong disconnection between a school and the neighborhood in which it resides (George & Shewey, 1994). Administrators and staff at the school view themselves as separate from the community, and members of the community view the school as an entity apart from the neighborhood.

Fortunately, this traditional approach to school–community relationships is changing. There is a realization that a school and a community have much to gain by working together. Community members have a social and fiscal investment in the activities of a school. The curriculum to which students are exposed, the manner of instruction, and what students are taught to value and avoid are viewed as school-based activities. As educators have gained knowledge regarding the processes that underlie learning, there has been a realization that learning takes place across contexts. Having consistent themes stressed at school, in the home, and throughout the community facilitates a more effective school.

However, school personnel cannot dictate what a community values; rather, they should reflect the community in its most positive sense. Using this tension between a school and a community in a constructive manner is the focus of school/community-based management. In this approach to managing a school, individuals from the community and the school work together to make strategic decisions about a school's activities. Community members include parents of children who are attending, will attend, or have previously attended the school, local civic leaders, business leaders, and individuals who have a stake in the outcomes produced by a school. These community members work with the school's administration and staff to set goals for the school, decide on strategies for achieving desired outcomes, and monitor the school's progress in achieving those goals. This approach has helped make schools more involved in their communities, has increased community participation in school activities, and facilitates the perception that the school is a resource for the local community (Sanders, 1996).

Many educators advocate that schools should focus on serving as a resource to the community, rather than vice versa (Sailor, 1996; Simeonsson & Simeonsson, 1999). An increasing number of models adopt such a perspective and view a school as a 24/7 (i.e., 24 hours a day, 7 days per week) resource for the community, instead of as a building that is open from 8 A.M. to 3 P.M., Monday through Friday. A school is seen as a resource center for the local community in the view of school–community partnerships. Many resources that families and other community members need are located at the school or nearby (e.g., mental health services, health care, family counseling). In addition, through feedback from community members, the school can serve as a meeting place and activity center for groups from the community.

By encouraging community involvement in school planning and decision making, a school becomes a reflection of the community in which it is situated and can serve as a resource for community members. This allows school personnel to have contact with and input from the school's neighborhood and allows the community to become more invested in the activities of the school. Typically, the result is an increase in the quality of educational services and greater use of school resources by the community (Swartz & Martin, 1997).

SCHOOL RESTRUCTURING

Middle schools have inherited their management structure from universities and colleges (see Chapter 3). Although this may have seemed an appropriate approach to school management, new information suggests that other approaches produce better outcomes (George & Shewey, 1994; Lounsbury, 1992). The process of moving from a higher education model to an alternative structure is referred to as *school restructuring*.

School restructuring involves determining a school's focus (i.e., its mission statement), how it will achieve those goals (i.e., its values statement), and the best arrangement to achieve those goals. This process involves creating *school teams* that concentrate teacher efforts on groups of students, rather than on traditional academic domains. For example, a middle school might decide to restructure itself so teachers from various curricular domains (math, social studies, health, English/language arts, special education, and science) work as a team for a certain number of students from a particular grade level. These teachers and students work together as a unit throughout the school year.

COMMUNITY VOLUNTEERS

Another way that community members can be involved in school life is through recruiting family members and other volunteers. This approach has at least two benefits. First, having additional adults working at the school results in increased personnel resources. Second, recruiting volunteers increases the involvement of the community in the activities of a school. Family members and community volunteers infuse the school with new ideas and allow additional activities to take place. Although family members, particularly parents of students, are the focus for recruiting community volunteers, additional resources are available for identifying potential contributors. Community groups that focus their efforts on volunteering are an effective resource.

Advocates of community volunteers suggest that these individuals can serve a number of roles within a school (Strom & Strom, 1999). For example, some can serve as instructional assistants to supplement the instruction of teachers. Others can work in areas that support instruction, such as the school office, library, cafeteria, or facilities maintenance. One of the best strategies for incorporating community volunteers into schools is to make use of their unique skills.

The second benefit of volunteerism for schools is increased inter-action between school personnel and community members. As with school/community-based management, the greater the interchange be-tween the school staff and community members, the more the school comes to reflect the values and character of its neighborhood. In addi-tion, community members experience a greater connection with and understanding of the school.

FOSTERING INCLUSION

There are other practices that educational administrators can take to foster inclusion. Three that merit particular attention are 1) promoting neighborhood schools, 2) providing staff development, and 3) demon-strating leadership in inclusive practices.

As mentioned previously, *neighborhood schools* is a concept that fo-cuses on which school students attend (Sailor, in press). This approach is important for promoting inclusive educational practices because it facilitates placement of students at schools in their zone in a non-categorical manner. In a neighborhood schools model, a school serves all students from its area. Advocates for neighborhood schools point out that this model enhances a school's presence in its community be-cause the school reflects the diversity of students who live in the com-munity and does not exclude students because of a disability.

Because education is a profession, ongoing staff development is a critical component for improving the skills of teachers and others. One of the barriers to implementing effective inclusive practices is the per-ception of teachers that they are required to learn additional skills. If teachers do not perceive themselves to have the abilities necessary to work in an inclusive school setting, then staff development becomes a necessary vehicle for increasing the skills of teachers and promoting a greater comfort level among school personnel.

Above all else, educational administrators should focus on leader-ship when increasing a school's capacity to be more inclusive. Although the concept of leadership is full of intangibles, it is, nevertheless, ac-knowledged that for effective school reform to take place, district and school administrators need to demonstrate support for those reforms. This entails supporting others' initiatives to make educational practices more inclusive, developing new initiatives, and modeling ways in which others should behave.

What does each of the practices discussed in this chapter have to do with creating inclusive middle schools? Each provides a context for pos-itive change. A school is a complex web of events, policies, and people that are necessarily interdependent. How one event may affect one group of people will have an impact on others at a school. For example, if one school team has a positive experience with inclusive practices, that experience will be communicated to others. This would result in people's viewing events and policies relating to inclusion more positively.

If schools are to change—and making a school more inclusive is a fundamental change—then the context needs to be set to enable and facilitate those changes. Educational administrators are at the foundation of those changes. By setting policies that allow teachers and others to pursue innovative practices, district and school administrators create an environment that will nurture and promote those changes. However, without administrative support, educational reforms are difficult for individuals or groups of individuals to carry out.

Reform efforts in the area of inclusive education require administrative supports. For example, district administrators who create school zoning policies that make neighborhood schools the preferred placement option promote inclusive practices and set in place a series of changes that make inclusion likely to succeed. Those changes include rearranging resources among schools and making sure that individual schools have the staffing to accommodate those changes. Another example is a building principal's decision that each school team will include a special educator as a core part of that group. This sets the context for general educators and special educators to work together and view each other as part of the same team, rather than as separate entities (as they have historically been perceived).

A school cannot become more inclusive without the clear and unambiguous support of educational administrators. The goal of this chapter has been to outline practices that have been demonstrated to promote inclusive educational practices. However, the practices reviewed are unique because they cannot occur without the explicit decision-making abilities that rest with educational administrators. District and building administrators cannot make educational reforms happen in a vacuum; they require setting a foundation for others to innovate and try new practices. However, educational reforms do not happen without the support and leadership of educational administrators.

"A person is a person through other persons." —*Bishop Desmond Tutu*

3

Building and Using Collaborative School Teams

Craig H. Kennedy
Douglas Fisher

"Most adolescents attend massive, impersonal schools, learn from unconnected and seemingly irrelevant curricula, know well and trust few adults in school, and lack access to [adequate emotional and behavioral supports]" (Carnegie Council on Adolescent Development, 1989, p. 13). This statement has been an accurate summary of school life for too many generations of middle school students. Counts tallied in the mid-1990s show that there are 13,543 middle schools in the United States serving 8,830,036 students, with an average of 652 students per school (Irvin, 1997; McEwin, Dickinson, & Jenkins, 1995). It has proved extremely difficult, if not impossible, to create personalized learning environments that provide each student with the supports he or she needs in such large settings.

The Carnegie Council's report noted the outcomes that can result from attempting to educate students in large numbers. They are exactly the types of outcomes that one wants to avoid with middle school students—alienation from adults, curriculum, and community. What can be done to overcome this problem given the reality of existing school buildings and school district structures? Tearing down older, larger buildings and constructing newer, smaller buildings is not feasible. Instead, administrators and staff within a school need to alter how they conceptualize what constitutes a *learning environment*.

Traditionally, as was noted in Chapter 2, middle schools were thought of as small-scale colleges or universities (Lounsbury, 1992). Educators in middle schools were grouped according to academic disciplines (e.g., English, history, art) just like a college or university. These departments were then integrated at a higher level by the administration. The educators in individual departments focused on the content that they were teaching (i.e., their curriculum); administrators focused on how the individual departments were coordinated as a whole; and students, it was assumed, would learn if exposed to the curriculum as they went from one course to the next.

Unfortunately, this higher education model of middle school structure has a number of demonstrated shortcomings. Several decades of research indicate that a higher education model is associated with the types of outcomes lamented in the Carnegie Council report (Clark & Clark, 1994; George & Shewey, 1994; Irvin, 1997). The higher education model takes preadolescent students from an elementary school setting in which most students attend the same class(es) with the same peers and teachers, often with integrated curricula, and places them in an environment designed for young adults attending a college or university. Students are suddenly in a much larger building (or series of buildings); they move from one class to another, which are taught by different teachers, who have little or no contact with each other; the curriculum differs across each class; no specific adult is responsible for supervising student achievement; and peers vary from one class to the next. Is it surprising, then, that students fall through the cracks in middle school? Current practices based on the higher education model of middle school structure seem to be unintentionally designed to produce such outcomes. Perhaps we should not be surprised that middle schools produce students who are alienated from adults, curriculum, and community.

What are alternative approaches to structuring middle school environments to promote academic and social development? Several proposed strategies have been conceptualized and tested, but the alternative with the strongest empirical support is school teams.

WHAT ARE SCHOOL TEAMS?

In the late 1960s, educators and researchers began exploring alternatives to higher education models for designing middle school learning environments. In essence, a learning environment is how people who are associated with a school define who, when, where, and how students are exposed to curriculum. As noted previously, higher education models group teachers in academic units. These individual units coordinate activities within themselves (e.g., sequencing math instruction across grade levels). During the school day, students move from one academic unit to another. The students come into contact with an adult from each academic unit, but little teacher-to-teacher interaction occurs across academic units. For a middle school with 600 students, during a typical school day, each teacher may see 150 students (six classes with 25 students each). However, no two teachers will see the same 150 students (see Figure 3.1).

When two teachers from within the same academic discipline talk about students, they are discussing entirely different groups of individuals (e.g., seventh-grade pre-algebra versus seventh-grade advanced algebra or sixth-grade pre-algebra versus seventh-grade pre-algebra).

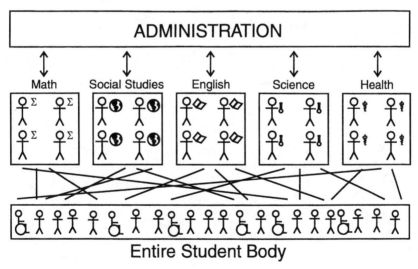

Figure 3.1.   An example of a traditional middle school structure. Professionals are arranged by academic discipline, and students move from one content area to another.

When two teachers from across academic disciplines talk about students, they may have approximately 35 students (of 600) in common. Those cross-department interactions typically are rare within a higher education model (Arhar, Johnston, & Markle, 1988). To overcome isolation among faculty and students, school teams can be used to provide smaller learning environments within a school.

School teams; also referred to as schools within a school, pods, interdepartmental teams, or interdisciplinary teams; divide middle schools into smaller clusters in which teachers and students interact within an integrated learning environment. Typically, these clusters have at least three defining characteristics: 1) students in the school are divided into groups of 100–200, 2) teachers are grouped among disciplines into teams (i.e., one teacher from each academic area is part of a team), and 3) one team of teachers is responsible for the social and academic outcomes of one group of students.

For example, a middle school with 600 students might be divided into four school teams composed of 150 students each and seven teachers (see Figure 3.2). The students within a school team come into contact with each of the teachers within their team on a daily basis (i.e., those teachers teach the students' classes), the students interact with each other in smaller, consistent groupings, teachers meet regularly to discuss the progress of students (whom each teacher in the team knows

School Teams Model

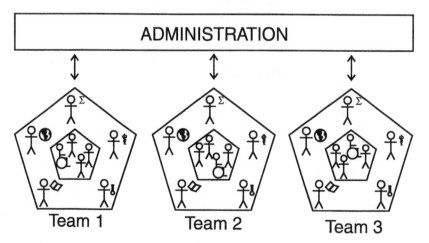

Figure 3.2.   An example of a middle school structure using a school teaming approach. Professionals are arranged by grade level, and students remain within a particular school team.

and sees daily), teachers can coordinate their teaching across disciplines based on common curricular themes, and teachers can collaboratively plan and implement support strategies for students who require additional assistance (e.g., gifted students, students at risk for behavior problems, students with a particular disability).

At their core, school teams create smaller learning environments within larger school building structures, allowing coordinated delivery of instruction across academic disciplines. School teams also allow more intensive contact among smaller groups of students and teachers, better monitoring of student progress, interdisciplinary teacher interaction, and creation of a sense of community among those individuals.

WHAT ARE KEY COMPONENTS OF SCHOOL TEAMS?

One way of illustrating the key components of school teams is to break down the concept into its structure and function. *Structure* is the organizational arrangement of a school that identifies important elements that compose school teams. *Function* is the actual activities of a school team that lead to specific teacher and student outcomes. Although any system is composed of the integration of structure and function, discussing each facet of a complete system allows for a better understanding of its constituent parts and their relation to each other (Coleman, 1990; March & Simon, 1993).

Structural Dimensions of School Teams

At least six distinct structural dimensions of a school team can be identified by reviewing contemporary middle school literature. Research suggests—although it does not conclusively or exhaustively demonstrate—that each of these dimensions appears to contribute to the overall success of school teams (Rottier, 1990) and, therefore, warrants inclusion in discussions of structural dimensions.

Interdepartmental Composition of School Teams
A hallmark of school teams is their composition by teachers across academic disciplines. Typically, this interdepartmental structuring is accomplished by having a representative from each core academic area, along with individuals with expertise in teaching students with specific needs. This means that representatives with specific content expertise in math, language arts, science, social sciences, health, as well as students with gifts and talents, specific learning disabilities, or significant disabilities are part of the team. This provides the team with the ability to work with a broad range of students across academic content areas. Put another way, this type of interdepartmental approach provides the team with both depth and breadth of teaching expertise.

Proportional Representation of the Student Body

Typically, each school team supports an equivalent number of students (distributing teacher-to-student ratios equitably across teachers and teams). The corollary of this is that student diversity be represented equally across school teams. Proportional representation of the entire student body at a school within each school team is an important dimension (Villa & Thousand, 1992). This means that school teams are *not* based on the heterogeneity of student characteristics (just as they are not based on a single academic discipline). Instead, each school team should be composed of students who represent the overall proportion of student characteristics in a particular school. For example, given current prevalence rates, a school team that has 150 students may have 10–20 identified as gifted and talented, 10–20 with specific learning disabilities, 2–3 with significant disabilities, and 15–30 who are at risk for school failure. Such an arrangement complements the interdepartmental structure of school teams and produces a number of positive student outcomes that will be elaborated on later in this book.

Teacher-to-Student Ratios

An important aspect of school teams is the opportunity for teachers and students to interact with each other on a regular basis. This allows teachers to get to know a small group of students well and note how individuals are developing academically and socially. Smaller teacher-to-student ratios also allow students to develop closer relationships with specific adults. Each of these benefits has been associated with improved student outcomes (see the section "What Outcomes Can School Teams Produce?"). Typically, researchers suggest that school teams be composed of 5–8 teachers and 100–200 students.

Grade Levels

Although a middle school, by definition, is composed of multiple grade levels, school teams often desegregate the student population by grade levels. In addition, school teams often follow students through the school from year to year. That is, the same group of teachers and students moves from one grade to the next to help ensure continuity from year to year. Although the linking of teachers and students has associated limitations, many teachers, administrators, and parents view this practice as desirable.

Selection of School Team Members

Two general strategies (or a combination) are used to select members for school teams. One approach is to allow teachers to *voluntarily* compose teams. A second approach is for school administrators to *appoint* team members. Advantages of the former approach include increased participation in the selection process and greater personal commitment; disadvantages include teams being constituted on the basis of personal preferences or friendships. Advantages of administrator appointment include flexibility in constructing team composition for teacher improvement and minimization of interpersonal conflict; disadvantages include decreased teacher participation. Not surprisingly, schools often select an intermediate approach to building school teams (Mac Iver, 1990). For example, administrators may specify to teachers what the overall structure of school teams will be (e.g., interdisciplinary composition, number of members) but allow teachers to select individual teams.

Team Leadership   Identifying a leadership structure within a school team is critical for effective team functioning (Mac Iver, 1990). Similar to the constitution of school teams, some mixture of self-selection and administrator-selected leadership roles is typically used. Mac Iver (1990) identified internally elected leaders and administrator-appointed leaders functioning within a fixed (e.g., one school year) or rotating basis (e.g., changing every quarter) as the most common approaches. This step is of particular importance because team leaders will be responsible for coordinating activities and communicating with other teams and school administrators.

Functional Dimensions of School Teams

Functional dimensions of school teams refer to the duties of these entities. This refers both to processes (e.g., which activities will be conducted) and to outcomes (e.g., what is accomplished as a result of specific actions). As noted by Baer (1993), an effective, functioning educational system requires the integration and assessment of both processes and outcomes into a set of activities to enable it to meet its goals. Several key functional dimensions are described in the following sections.

Team Members' Roles and Responsibilities   Along with identifying a leadership structure, school team members need to identify team members' roles and responsibilities. Responsibilities that need to be identified may include teaching assignments, how students are grouped, when meetings occur, which commonalities and differences will exist across classrooms, selection of curriculum materials, and opportunities for interdisciplinary instruction and curriculum integration (Alexander & George, 1981). In addition, explicit expectations about meeting attendance, taking and reporting of minutes, the chairing of meetings, and similar matters need to be clarified at the outset of team formation.

Planning Times and Goal Setting   There is a close link between planning time and improved educational outcomes (Mac Iver, 1990). Although the reasons for this association are more complex than space allows, the opportunity for professionals to meet and discuss issues that relate to student education is critical. One of the benefits of school teams is that a small group of teachers collaborate together over time with a specific group of students. An important first step is scheduling planning times with administrators. Typically, school teams meet once or twice a week for approximately 1 hour, with additional meeting times reserved for ad hoc committees developed by the team (see Ames & Miller, 1994, for scheduling tips).

Planning times focus on identifying specific goals for the team to achieve and developing strategies for achieving them. Initial meetings may focus on which goals need to be achieved and the time frame for achieving those goals. Once these preliminaries are identified, planning time can focus on developing concrete strategies for meeting goals (see Sections II and III of this book for an extended discussion of educational strategies). Although it is a cliché, an important step in setting goals is to specify in clear, unambiguous terms what will be achieved and when. In addition, the individual(s) responsible for achieving specific goals should be identified in team meetings. Once goals and strategies have been developed and implemented, the team is responsible for monitoring progress toward meeting goals and suggesting opportunities for modifying, maintaining, or terminating activities in relation to the goal's status. For example, if a particular strategy has been implemented and the desired changes have not resulted, then the team needs to work together to develop an alternative or modified strategy.

One area in which teams emphasize setting goals is the *curriculum*. A great deal of setting goals focuses on integrating the curriculum across disciplines within the team, coordinating lessons, identifying accommodations and modifications that specific students may require, and planning instructional strategies. A second area focuses on setting goals for *students*. This occurs individually, for classes, and for the team's cohort of students as a whole. For example, goals could include positive behavior support plans for a particular student, a class meeting, a homework completion goal, or improving the attendance of students throughout the school team. Finally, goals should be set for the functions of the team itself. Areas of focus often include meeting regularly, making efficient use of meeting time, ensuring the effectiveness of instructional activities, securing satisfaction of team members with processes and outcomes, and improving team members' participation in team activities.

Integrating the Curriculum   A central role for school teams is ensuring that each discipline represented on the team is working on a similar curriculum. Multiple benefits accrue when the different core subjects work together to embed goals across subject areas (see Chapter 4). For example, each class that students attend may be working within a consistent thematic structure (e.g., space exploration) in which aspects of math, English, science, social studies, and health are integrated into each class.

Monitoring Student Progress   In the early 1960s, Ogden Lindsley introduced educators to the benefits of monitoring student development and how to use that information to make instructional decisions (Lindsley, 1991). Lindsley demonstrated that by making teachers more aware of how individual students were progressing (or not progressing), substantial gains in student achievement could result. One of the values of a school team is that it allows each of the adults involved in educating a student to assess, evaluate, and note the student's development and work as a group. For example, a student's performance may begin to taper off in math. Knowing how he or she is performing in other subjects provides important information to his or her teachers—does the student need additional tutoring in the current math content, or is he or she suddenly experiencing problems across subjects that might be a symptom of a larger problem? Chapters 6 and 9 of this book deal explicitly with techniques for monitoring student progress; however, this concept is foundational and is implicit in much of the text.

Student Advocacy   An important component of effective school teams is the use of teacher advocates or teacher advisors (Linn & Songer, 1991; Ziegler & Mulhall, 1994). The goal is to have each student on a team linked with a specific teacher. The teacher is responsible for maintaining regular contact with the students with whom he or she is working (typically, between 15 and 30 students from the team), monitoring their social and academic progress, and providing an interpersonal monitoring process for assessing signs of concern regarding student performance. Typically, these meetings are based on homeroom or study hall assignments.

What Outcomes Can School Teams Produce?

The practices recommended in this book are based on research findings. These studies serve as guideposts for what constitutes education's recommended practices. What does the research literature say about the pluses and minuses of developing and implementing school teams? There are several facets, as well as caveats, in the literature on school teaming. Fortunately, the research is sufficiently developed to make relatively clear suggestions about specific practices and which costs and benefits likely will result from their adoption by a school and its teachers.

Creating Smaller Learning Environments   A number of positive outcomes, as well as suggestions for structuring teams, comes from the contemporary research literature. Researchers have documented that students perceive schools that have interdisciplinary teams as being more supportive of social and academic progress (Arhar et al., 1988; McLaughlin, Talbert, Kahne, & Powell, 1990). In addition, teachers and students have reported that school teams are associated with improved school climates (Epstein & Mac Iver, 1990). These findings suggest that the individuals at a school who are using interdisciplinary teams view the school as creating smaller niches for teachers and students to interact. Additional research suggests that most teams are composed of three to five individuals and that creating larger teams leads to scheduling difficulties and other forms of inefficiency (Clark & Clark, 1992; Mac Iver, 1990; Martin, 1999). Interestingly, studies suggest no differential outcomes for teams that were selected by teachers versus teams that were selected by administrators (Mac Iver, 1990). However, data clearly indicate that the appointment of a leader(s) is important in creating an effective and cohesive team (Mac Iver, 1990; Martin, 1999).

Improved Professional Development   A consistent finding among researchers is that the use of school teams results in improved decision making by teachers. That is, teachers become better at identifying problems and implementing effective solutions within and among classrooms. Part of these effects may be due to increased planning time and improved goal setting when teachers work in teams (Cohen, 1981; Mac Iver, 1990; Merenbloom, 1991). These improvements are indicated by improved teaching practices (Arhar, 1992; Mac Iver, 1990) and more positive social relationships among team teachers, as well as with their students (Arhar, 1992; Midgley & Edelin, 1998). School administrators and teachers also report greater productivity and work satisfaction in schools that use teams (Little, 1982; Rosenholtz, 1989). A change related to this improved professional development resulting from teaming is an increase in collegiality and reciprocal advice giving and receiving among team members (Rosenholtz, 1989). Overall, school teaming seems to be associated with improved professional development (Lieberman, 1990).

Improved Student Performance   What happens to students when they are placed in school teams? Effects are observed across a number of student performance indicators, as well as effective variables. One consistent finding is that students report having stronger social relationships, not only with other students in their team but also with teachers (Arhar, Johnston, & Markle, 1989; George & Oldaker, 1985; Midgley & Edelin, 1998). This is likely related to decreases in school drop out rates and referrals for discipline problems that are observed when school teams are in place (Epstein & Mac Iver, 1990; George & Oldaker, 1985). A number of studies also demonstrate improvements in a range of academic areas (Epstein & Mac Iver, 1990; Little, 1982; Mac Iver, 1990). All these findings have been reported to occur at a greater level for heterogeneous groups that include a full range of learners, as opposed to homogeneous grouping practices (Rosenholtz, 1989). However, the range of benefits that seems to result from school teams tends to have a larger impact on students' social development than on their academic development (Midgley & Edelin, 1998). In general, the data on student outcomes favor school teaming.

Promoting Greater Diversity   Finally, there is emerging evidence that school teams help promote more diverse interpersonal relationships among students. There is evidence of more diverse social relationships based on ethnic, linguistic, and cultural backgrounds (Damico, Bell, & Green, 1981). Research also has shown that students with disabilities are accepted and more embedded in middle schools that use a teaming approach (Johnson, Johnson, & Holubec, 1986; Kennedy et al., 1997). A corollary of these findings is that school teams are associated with decreases in student, teacher, and family reports of student alienation at school (Calabrese & Seldin, 1987; McPartland, 1987). Together, these findings suggest that the social structures that are put into place using school teams allow for a greater range of friendships and acquaintances to emerge when compared to more traditional approaches to schooling.

Cautionary Notes   A review of the research on school teams would be remiss if it did not note shortcomings and limitations (Clark & Clark, 1994; George & Shewey, 1994; Hoy & Sabo, 1997; Irvin, 1992). First and foremost, school teaming involves change in personal and professional roles and can be threatening to teachers and staff. If this perceived threat is great enough and teacher resistance is strong, then the teaming approach itself, as well as its positive outcomes, tend not to be realized. A second limitation of school teams is an increase in the required planning time. As a result of the interdisciplinary nature of teams, a greater amount of meeting time and effort, at least initially, is involved in coordinating the curriculum, as well as setting goals and student monitoring. Third, because more teacher time is focused on integrating curriculum, setting goals, and monitoring student outcomes, there can be a decrease in the amount of instructional time that students receive. However, researchers still need to clarify the interrelations between the quantity of instructional time and the quality of instruction; more may not always be better. Finally, as in all professional activities, tact, respect for others, and social skills are necessary for team functioning. Many school teams have reported failure as a result of one or more individuals being unable or unwilling to adopt a team-based approach to instruction and the social requirements it entails.

Kaneohe Middle School

Experience has shown that each middle school adjusts the various structures and functions of school teams to the unique characteristics of a particular school. However, this story from Kaneohe Middle School (KMS) offers an example of how one school developed and implemented a school team model. KMS is located on the northern side of Oahu, Hawaii. Students come to KMS primarily from the communities that surround the school. Those communities represent a range of socioeconomic conditions, such as middle-income families from the nearby military base, families on public assistance, and affluent professional households. In addition, students at this school come from a range of cultural and ethnic backgrounds. The school has approximately 900 students who represent a range of academic functioning, including 81 students with learning or moderate disabilities and 9 students with more significant disabilities. The school is composed of sixth, seventh, and eighth grades.

KMS previously had been structured using a higher education model with groups of teachers aligned by academic discipline and students moving among departments during the school day. Class sizes at KMS are relatively large, typically between 30 and 35 students. There are a total of 30 teachers at the school, with 25 teachers having credentials in general education and 5 teachers having credentials in special education (including gifted and talented). Historically, drop out rates, erratic school attendance, and gang membership were persistent concerns for students and teachers. The school's climate often was characterized as impersonal, with feelings of disengagement on the campus.

Concerned about the school's climate, a committee composed of KMS teachers and administrators, parents, and interested community members was created to explore ways of improving school climate, student outcomes, and teacher satisfaction. A year-long meeting process resulted in a plan to implement a school teaming approach. The faculty, administration, and community agreed that it would be best for the school to implement school teams beginning in the fall.

Five teaching teams with six members each were established by the administration and faculty representatives. Each team contained a specialist in English and language arts, math, science, social studies, special education, and auxiliary programs (e.g., art, music, physical education). The composition of students among teams also was representative of the school. This entailed that six teachers on a team were responsible for 180 students. Three of the teams were grade level specific; two of the teams had students from adjacent grade levels.

A Hawaiian state policy specified that all middle school students attend seven periods of instruction per day, along with lunch and recess. Because of this policy, no changes in block scheduling or other creative scheduling were considered. Teachers agreed to meet once a week, after school, for the first semester and then switch to biweekly meetings after that. In return, administrators created a flex-time structure for teachers attending the after-school meetings. Each team self-selected a leader who would rotate from year to year. Team leaders then met once per month as a group with administrators, as well as on an as-needed basis. The principal attended one team's meeting each week.

The results of this process generally were positive. Although a few teachers were concerned about the extra meeting time and were unable to focus exclusively on their academic area, the process was smoothly implemented. Because KMS was collaborating on research relating to inclusive education with faculty and staff members from a local university, the teachers were able to use these individuals to serve as external evaluators.

Subjectively, it had been noted that teachers were more aware of each other's activities, the curriculum had been realigned and was more interdisciplinary, teachers had gotten to know the students in their teams very well, and the climate of the school had improved. These subjective changes were reflected in improvements in the school's scores on a recommended practices checklist (Kennedy et al., 1997). In general, KMS had raised its scores on a number of variables related to effective schooling and student outcomes (see Table 3.1). In particular, KMS substantially improved across interdisciplinary teaming, school climate, and student participation categories.

These external observations were consistent with how teachers and administrators at KMS felt about the process. Overall, school personnel, students, and community members were pleased with the changes that had been associated with school teams, so the school opted to continue the process and make refinements when required.

Importance of School Teams

School teams are not a new idea. Lounsbury and other advocates for improving middle schools have been noting their importance since the 1960s. However, it was not until the 1980s that clear evidence was available regarding their effectiveness. At the end of the 1990s, the evidence in support of school teaming was stronger than ever, but school teams,

Table 3.1.   Scores on a best practices checklist for Kaneohe Middle School (KMS)

	End of previous year	End of school teaming year
Home–school partnerships	75%	90%
Quality of instruction	72%	84%
Interdisciplinary teaming	43%	91%
School climate	49%	82%
Student participation	53%	79%

Percentages represent the proportion of best practices demonstrated at the school.

despite their many advantages, are not a panacea. Instead, they are a foundation that facilitates other innovative practices being put into place. School teams are at the heart of middle school educational reform for a good reason—they provide a necessary set of conditions that allows and perhaps encourages school improvement efforts. However, school teams do come at a cost. In part, the costs are breaking with past traditions associated with school structures based on a higher education model. Those costs are largely historical and can easily be discarded as part of an evolutionary process. Other costs cannot easily be dismissed and, in fact, need to be addressed as part of the planning process for developing school teams. Administrators and teachers need to agree on how to arrange for increased planning and meeting time in a manner that is equitable for all involved. Similarly, it takes time for the people involved to learn how to function within an interdisciplinary team structure. Finally, change itself is difficult and cannot be effectively carried out by administrative or staff decree; it is a process—a process that requires collaboration and communication among adults and students. Despite their costs, however, school teams are a proven approach to helping schools improve themselves and are worth the effort in light of student, teacher, and school outcomes.

II

INCLUSIVE MIDDLE SCHOOL CURRICULUM

"It is wiser to find out than to suppose."
—Mark Twain

4

Access to the
Middle School Core Curriculum

Douglas Fisher
Craig H. Kennedy

Curriculum has been described in many ways (Posner, 1995). Some people talk about curriculum as the content that is covered in a specific class. Others maintain that curriculum also is the instructional strategies that teachers use. The term *curriculum* is used to describe a course of study. In other words, curriculum is viewed as both the content and the methods that a teacher uses to plan and conduct his or her class. This chapter focuses on the content of the curriculum and the ways in which students with disabilities gain access to the general education curriculum. However, before curriculum, accommodations, and modifications can be discussed, the standards that are established for all students must be examined.

WHY EDUCATIONAL STANDARDS?

The national effort to improve the educational achievement of America's school children is grounded in the establishment of rigorous learning standards at every level of elementary and secondary education (Roach, 1999). In developing a standards-based system, policymakers and educators hope to refocus teaching and learning on a common understanding of what communities expect students to know and be able to do as a result of their public school experience (Tucker & Codding, 1998). Once established, the standards provide the foundation for deciding what to teach and how to assess students' progress.

Curriculum frameworks are outlines that establish benchmarks for curriculum content at the various grade levels, thus providing the broad context from which districts develop their specific curricula. These benchmarks establish the goals and objectives for students at each grade level. In some states, these frameworks merely provide voluntary guidance to local districts as they develop their curriculum. In other states, the frameworks provide the foundation for new statewide assessment systems, as well as guidance for textbook approval, curriculum priorities, and instructional strategies.

The proponents of standards-based reform maintain that if high, rigorous standards are created for all students—and clearly communicated to educators, students, family members, business leaders, policymakers, and the community at large—then a coordinated effort that focuses on increased achievement can be mounted (NASBE, 1996; Tucker & Codding, 1998). The intended result is that all students, from all socioeconomic backgrounds (including those with limited English proficiency and those with disabilities) will achieve their desired goals (McDonnell & McLaughlin, 1997). In other words, the expectations for all students are increased and the entire system is focused on helping students achieve those higher expectations.

IMPACT OF STANDARDS-BASED
REFORM ON STUDENTS WITH DISABILITIES

Intuitively, many people think that increasing educational standards ought to benefit all students. Parents and educators have long believed that raising expectations results in higher achievement for students with disabilities. Educators often believe that if local school officials want to increase the percentage of students who score in the proficient or mastery categories on state assessments, they should increase all students' access to rigorous academic classes and effective teachers. It is encouraging that adopting higher expectations for students leads to the dissolution of low-track special education classes such as applied English, functional math, and science skills. Perhaps even greater numbers of students with disabilities might be enrolled in college preparatory classes, thus broadening their career options and their potential earning power as adults.

Furthermore, educators understand that adopting high standards for all students should promote the elimination of tracking and the inclusion of students with disabilities using common learning standards for all students (Fisher, Sax, & Pumpian, 1999). In the context of standards-based reform, the curriculum is viewed as a unifying vehicle to ensure that a variety of students master the same information.

What is the relationship among state standards, curriculum frameworks, and local practice? The national effort to improve the educational achievement of America's school children is grounded in the establishment of rigorous learning standards at every level of elementary and secondary education. In developing a standards-based system, policymakers hope to refocus teaching and learning on a common understanding of what communities expect students to know and be able to do as a result of their public school experience. Once established, the standards provide the foundation for curriculum development, or, in the current parlance, designing curriculum frameworks.

Unfortunately, there is an unfavorable scenario for describing the impact of standards-based reform on students with disabilities. What if states develop learning standards that do not reflect the needs of students with disabilities or others who traditionally have been only marginally included in the educational system? What if different standards are developed for different kinds of students—honors expectations for honors students, special education expectations for special education students, and so forth? If students with disabilities are not considered in the development of general standards or the design of curriculum frameworks or if their test scores are not included in an aggregate district score, an even more segregated system of education might evolve. It is possible that schools would do more tracking, and students with disabilities would have less access to high-level curriculum than they do now. Fewer students with disabilities might qualify for a high school diploma, and their future educational and career choices would continue to be limited.

EIGHT ELEMENTS OF CURRICULUM AND INSTRUCTION

Educator Cheryl Jorgensen (1998) maintained that success in developing effective, inclusive learning experiences for all students emanates from teachers' beliefs and philosophy about teaching and learning, from the curriculum content guidelines adopted by the state and school district, and from teachers' utilization of a particular set of unit and lesson design principles.

Determining what and how to teach all students—the content of the curriculum—requires an examination of more than just the body of knowledge that currently exists in particular academic disciplines. All students, including those with disabilities, need to learn three types of skills:

1. Dispositions and habits of mind, such as inquisitiveness, diligence, collaboration, work habits, tolerance, and critical thinking
2. Content area knowledge in science, social studies, language arts, computers, the arts, and so forth
3. Basic academic skills, such as reading, writing, and mathematics

Educators concerned primarily with teaching students with disabilities might wish that all schools would develop their curriculum to address all three of these skill areas. If they did, it would be possible for any school to address any student's priority learning goals. No school would be too academic, too vocational, or too devoted to the basics for students with disabilities. This could be accomplished by setting high standards for all students.

Considering the variability in curriculum and instruction from district to district and from school to school, it is recommended that all teachers use some common curricular elements to design teaching and learning experiences that transcend philosophical differences, resulting in a learning environment that challenges and supports all students. Onosko and Jorgensen (1998) identified eight such curricular elements. A brief definition of each follows.

Element #1: A Central Unit Issue, Problem, or Question

Structuring a unit of study around an issue, problem, or essential question creates a framework for the learning experience and provides direction and coherence. In a standards-based curriculum, these central unit issues are generated by teachers with the standards firmly in mind. In an ancient civilization unit, for example, the issue might be "Are the Greeks still with us today?" In this unit, students can demonstrate their mastery of several content standards, depending on the particular activities and products the teacher has planned. Students can illustrate that they understand the concepts of continuity and change in history, as well as principles and processes of social systems (e.g., the Olympics). They also should be able to comprehend and assess the content and artistic aspects of oral and visual presentations.

When all students in a classroom are focused on addressing a common question, differences in learning styles and abilities are less important than the commonality of all students' comprehending meaning in the content area, albeit in a personalized way. Well-crafted essential questions or problems offer challenge and accessibility to all students.

Element #2: Unit "Grabber"

Beginning each major unit of study with a highly motivating *grabber* or kick-off activity can help engage all students. Inclusive classrooms are composed of a variety of students, including those who already know a good deal of the subject matter and can express their knowledge well, students who know a lot but have difficulty showing it, students who have no prior experience with or knowledge about the topic at hand, and students who are more interested in alternative rock music than in U.S. history. A first-day activity that proposes a provocative question to students (e.g., What is worth fighting for?), which allows them to interact with someone who lived the history (e.g., a Holocaust survivor) or that provides a simulation (e.g., a simulated stock market crash game), is another element of effective, inclusive curriculum design.

Element #3: Learning Experiences that Link

All students need to have explicit connections made among individual daily learning experiences. Teachers must ensure that daily activities logically build students' knowledge throughout the unit to enable them to use the body of newly acquired knowledge to answer the overall unit question. For example, three activities that might accomplish this goal are 1) identifying various viewpoints or positions regarding the unit's central issue or problem, 2) identifying key concepts, events, or people related to the issue under consideration, and 3) identifying and answering questions that need to be considered to address intelligently the problem or issue.

Element #4: Richly Detailed Source Material

The use of richly detailed source material that represents a variety of student learning styles and intelligence ensures that each student in the class has access to the knowledge base about the topic being studied. Too often, teachers put students with reading difficulties at a distinct disadvantage from the start by failing to augment print-based information sources. For example, most students would better understand a lecture on World War II and the Holocaust if the teacher were to include a videotape of a survivor, actual letters written during the time (e.g., *The Diary of Anne Frank*), and personal interviews with his or her family members who lived during the war.

Element #5: Varied Learning Formats

When teachers use a variety of teaching formats, such as cooperative groups, whole-class instruction, student pairs, Socratic dialogue, labs, and teacher–student conferencing, the probability increases that each student's learning style will be addressed. Varying the instructional format lessens boredom and predictability. This gives teachers more opportunities to get up close and personal with each student to assess progress, to analyze the difficulties he or she is having with the materials, to correct mistakes and misunderstandings, and ultimately to adjust future teaching and learning experiences based on that feedback.

Element #6: Multiple Assessments

To ensure powerful student learning, teachers need to monitor and assess students' progress throughout the unit, not just at the end. The greater diversity found in the inclusive classroom makes the need for periodic assessment even more critical. For this reason, multiple assessments are important elements of inclusive unit design. Assessment systems are more fully described in Chapter 6.

Element #7: Varied Modes of Expression

Intelligence is composed of many different kinds of abilities and talents. Teachers traditionally tend to emphasize verbal-linguistic and logical-mathematical intelligences to the exclusion of most other talents. Teachers in inclusive classrooms need to design instructional and assessment activities that tap into a variety of intelligences. For example, in a unit on inventions that uses all of the students' intelligence, musically inclined students study the science behind the invention of electronic music, spatially smart students build or draw a new invention, and students with strong linguistic and interpersonal intelligence form a discussion group and write policy briefs on the use of inventions that are intended to cause harm, such as the atomic bomb.

Element #8: Culminating Projects

Culminating projects provide students with opportunities to demonstrate their understanding of the unit's central issue, problem, or question through a public presentation. When teachers provide choices for how students can present their final exhibition, including options for written papers, demonstrations, oral presentations, and building models, each student has the opportunity to use his or her favored learning style.

WHAT WOULD A
STANDARDS-BASED LESSON LOOK LIKE?

Some people maintain that students with disabilities can use the general education curriculum in a self-contained special education classroom. However, few special education teachers received training in curriculum content in their preservice programs or have attended district-sponsored professional development programs on standards-based instruction. Hence, access to the curriculum for students with disabilities is dependent on access to the general education classroom. The following example of Mr. Lee, a middle school teacher, helps to explain standards and their impact on students.

Standards in Mr. Lee's Classroom

When he plans a unit, Mr. Lee reviews the state curriculum framework, the district standards that have been approved by his school board, and the content standards published by national organizations such as the National Council on Social Studies and the National Council of Teachers of English. Mr. Lee recently designed a specific unit related to World War II to meet the English and social studies curriculum standards for his students. This unit addressed several social studies themes, including culture, global connections, people who supply our needs, and geography. The unit addressed the social studies goal in the following way (Kendall & Marzano, 1997):

- *Understand the causes and course of World War II, the character of the war at home and abroad, and the war's reshaping of the United States' role in world affairs*

In addition, this unit addressed a number of English and language arts standards:

- *Demonstrate competence in the general skills and strategies of the writing process*
- *Use grammatical and mechanical conventions in written compositions*
- *Gather and use information for research purposes*
- *Demonstrate competence in the general skills and strategies for reading a variety of literary and informational texts*
- *Demonstrate competence in speaking and listening as tools for learning*

After identifying the standards, Mr. Lee follows a four-step process in creating the unit of study for his students. The four components include identifying 1) books and other information sources, 2) instructional arrangements, 3) projects and class activities, and 4) assessments and final projects.

Step 1: Books and Other Information Sources

Mr. Lee selects the Newbery award–winning book *Number the Stars*, a book about a Jewish girl who hides from the Nazi's during the Holocaust, by Lois Lowry (1989) as the focus book for the unit. In addition, he identifies sections of the social studies textbook for students to read, web sites and videos that are appropriate for children to view, and additional books on this theme for his classroom library for students to read during silent reading. Mr. Lee identifies a wide range of books on the topic, including books that are interesting for less fluent readers. He does this to ensure that every student can find a book that is instructional but not frustrating. He adds to his classroom library a number of books on this topic, including *Twenty and Ten* (Bishop, 1952), *When Hitler Stole Pink Rabbit* (Kerr, 1971), *The Upstairs Room* (Reiss, 1972), *Star of Fear, Star of Hope* (Hoestlandt, 1993), and *A Multicultural Portrait of World War II* (Wright, 1994).

Step 2: Instructional Arrangements

As his next step in designing the unit, Mr. Lee identifies instructional arrangements. Mr. Lee uses whole-class, small-group instruction, individual teacher–student conferences, and cooperative groups in his class. As he arranges for this 2-week time period, Mr. Lee drafts daily lessons based on the standards he is teaching. For example, Mr. Lee decides to read aloud to the students every other chapter of *Number the Stars*. They will partner to read the opposite chapters. He also decides to use learning centers with cooperative groups. Each center focuses on an aspect of World War II and engages students via one of the multiple learning styles. For example, one of the centers involves journal writing based on actual diaries from the Holocaust. Another center focuses on geography and involves mapping the progress of the war based on listening to actual radio broadcasts recorded during World War II.

Step 3: Projects and Class Activities

Mr. Lee uses writing journals, retelling inventories, and comprehension questions to check his students' understanding of the material throughout the unit. He is interested in projects and class activities that provide him information that he can use to alter his instruction. For example, during the World War II unit, Mr. Lee asks his students to maintain personal reflection journals. Mr. Lee uses these journals to gain an understanding of his students' thinking about the text, as well as to identify whose literacy skills may need attention. He also develops a number of class activities that involve speaking and viewing. For example, one day students produce their own radio show on the events thus far in the war. Students are assigned to various roles such as producer, announcer, investigator, interviewer, and interviewees such as civilians, military officers, and elected officials.

Step 4: Assessments and Final Projects

During this unit, Mr. Lee uses a culminating project to evaluate his entire curriculum program and to determine whether the instructional methods he selected were appropriate for his students. This final project is tiered, which means that students can select from a menu of possible projects for this unit. Some of the students interview people who lived during World War II and present their reports in writing and orally. Other students script a performance event about the Holocaust and visually present the information that they learned. Still others write poems or songs about their reaction to studying World War II and present them in writing and orally to the class. One student is interested in the chronology of the war and creates a visual time line with an accompanying map to show the world as it became more dominated by Germany.

It is important to note that Romielle, a student with significant disabilities in Mr. Lee's second-period class, participates in the World War II unit with the support of her classmates and the special education teacher. She reads the book using pictures, listens to a tape-recorded version that another student in the class has made, creates her story map using magazine pictures like everyone else, and is assessed on her own learning. She works with a group of students on the culminating project, in which they produce a play about World War II and how people were treated. Romielle uses her speech output device to perform her parts and picture communication symbols that match the story that the group has written (see Chapter 7 for more information on the use of technology in instruction).

In Mr. Lee's fourth-period class, the special educator supports Rory, a student with a learning disability. Rory needs fewer supports than Romielle to be successful. The text is more difficult than he is used to, but the read-aloud and partner-reading activities ensure that Rory understands the content. He also likes listening to the book on tape at home while reading the text of the same book. Rory often makes spelling mistakes and is frustrated with writing. Having access to a computer with a spell-check program and to classwide peer editing changes Rory's attitude. In addition, he is interested in how people were treated during World War II and, hence, has a lot of information about which he wants to write. His motivation on the topic, with instructional accommodations, helps him to overcome his traditional frustration with writing. Rory also needs some assistance with his final project. Given his interest in the treatment of people, he interviews people who lived during World War II and presents his investigative reporting to the entire class.

HOW DO STUDENTS WITH DISABILITIES PARTICIPATE IN STANDARDS-BASED LESSONS?

Students with disabilities are entitled to a continuum of supports in the general education class as part of their individualized education program (IEP). These include 1) personal supports such as special education teachers, paraprofessionals, peers, and related services staff, 2) accommodations and modifications to the curriculum to ensure access, and 3) instructional and assistive technology such as computers, software programs, pencil grips, ramps, and speech output devices (Castagnera, Fisher, Rodifer, & Sax, 1998).

Mr. Lee's expertise in the content areas is invaluable to students with and without disabilities. His ability to design lessons that are based on the standards and have a variety of accommodations and modifications further ensures student success. Students with and without disabilities learn best when the lessons are developed with a range of students' needs in mind as Mr. Lee has done (see Jorgensen, 1998, for additional examples).

Creating Accommodations and Modifications for Specific Students

As teachers become more familiar and comfortable with inclusive education, they often formalize a process for supporting students with disabilities in their general education classes. Over the years, the forms will change and can be expected to continue to evolve. Many students require curriculum accommodations and modifications based on their individual abilities. The remainder of this chapter outlines the process that is used to do this. Additional student examples can be found in Castagnera et al. (1998).

Teachers consider three interrelated supports for every lesson: technology, curriculum modifications, and specialized support staff (see Figure 4.1; see also Chapters 7 and 8). Students require varying levels of support in terms of curriculum and personnel. Each class and lesson is unique and requires that teachers plan accordingly. Overutilization of these supports constitutes a very restrictive intervention for the student and a situation in which the student learns little. Underutilization of these supports constitutes dumping and a situation in which the student may be set up to fail.

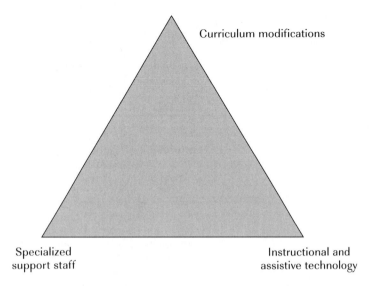

Curriculum modifications

Specialized
support staff

Instructional and
assistive technology

Figure 4.1.   Triangle of support for inclusive lesson planning. (From Fisher, D., Sax, C., & Pumpian, I. [1999]. *Inclusive high schools: Learning from contemporary classrooms.* Baltimore: Paul H. Brookes Publishing Co.; reprinted by permission.)

Assignments and lesson plans initially are developed around the core curriculum and the content and performance standards for the class. When general education teachers provide multilevel instruction, adapting the lesson plan may not be necessary. This type of instruction allows the students a variety of ways to demonstrate knowledge while continuing to meet the requirements of the class. For example, the whole class may be responsible for creating a concept map of the plant unit in science. Romielle and Rory do not need any accommodations or modifications for this assignment. As the group pictorially demonstrates their learning on a large piece of chart paper, Romielle participates with the group by selecting pictures for the concept map by looking at the picture of her choice.

The amount and type of curriculum modification depend significantly on the lesson plan and the specific content of the class (see Table 4.1 for a summary of the range of modification options). As in the example of the concept map, the assignment is left *as is* for the student with an IEP. Over the past several years, with a focus on inclusive curriculum design (Jorgensen, 1998), more and more students are supported in this fashion. Some students, however, need *accommodations* to the lesson. For example, teachers may enlarge the type or request a braille version of a paper. Some students need *modifications* to the lesson. The type of modifications varies; some students complete the *same assignment only less.* For example, on a multiple-choice test for social studies, the number

Table 4.1.   Curriculum design

Differentiated instruction	Provides for multiple ways of presenting and teaching information to students. When this type of instructional design is provided, the assignments remain unchanged. More information on differentiated instruction can be found in Chapter 6.
Accommodation	A change made to the teaching or testing procedures to provide a student with access to information and to create an equal opportunity to demonstrate knowledge and skills. Accommodations do not change the instructional level, content, or performance criteria for meeting the standards. Examples of accommodations include enlarging the print, providing oral versions of tests, and using calculators.
Modification	A change in what a student is expected to learn and/or demonstrate. Although a student may be working on modified course content, the subject area remains the same as for the rest of the class. Examples include *same only less* (the assignment remains the same except the number of items is reduced), *streamlining the curriculum* (the assignment is reduced in size to emphasize the key points), *same activity/infused objective* (the assignment remains the same but additional components are added), and *curriculum overlapping* (the assignment for one class may be completed in another class).

of answers from which to choose for each question is reduced from five to two. If these modifications are not appropriate, teachers begin to *streamline the curriculum*. This means that the student will be responsible for key aspects of the assignment, but not necessarily for the whole assignment. For example, when a research paper is assigned in English, Romielle completes an outline using magazine pictures or picture communication symbols. Her essay on *Hatchet* (Paulsen, 1987) was completed using picture communication symbols with words. In addition, teachers may use the *same activity with an infused objective*. In Romielle's science class, she uses a switch to operate a speech output device and specialized equipment for standing at the lab tables with her partners. Finally, teachers *overlap curriculum*. Romielle and her peer Jessica completed work for their social studies class during computer lab, a one-term requirement for all students.

Infused Skills Grid   Teachers will find the infused skills grid useful in determining what and where to teach (see Figure 4.2). This grid shows how functional skills can be infused into the daily routine of the student. Targeted skills, generated from the student profile, and family interviews are listed across the top of the grid. Listed along the left-hand column are the classes and activities that occur throughout the student's day. A checkmark is placed in each box to indicate a time period in which the skill will occur. For example, Romielle's family wanted Romielle to learn how to dress herself, so a checkmark was placed in the physical education column, as this is an appropriate time period during which she had opportunities to practice dressing skills. Her family also was concerned about Romielle's learning to answer who, what, when, where, and why questions. This skill was addressed throughout all of her classes.

Unit Planner and Weekly Assignment Sheet   Teachers can organize their unit with the Unit Lesson Plan (see Figure 4.3 for an example in the subject of science). General education teachers indicate the major unit objectives, materials needed, instructional arrangements, projects and activities, and assessments. The completed form is then given to the inclusion support teacher (i.e., the special educator who consults with the general educator), who in turn reviews each area and determines the level of modification or support needed. For example, Romielle's seventh-grade English class was assigned *Hatchet* (Paulsen, 1987) as part of a unit on survival. The English teacher selected a variety of printed materials, a video, and related activity sheets and organized instruction into individual assignments, small-group work, whole-class participation, and student performances. Students in the class read related poetry and stories, completed homework assignments, and performed an interpretation based on the novel. Assessments for this unit included the videotaped interpretation, an objective test, and a final essay. All of this information is recorded on the left-hand side of the unit plan form. Using the accommodation and modification processes described previously, the inclusion support teacher completes the right side of the form, providing appropriate accommodations and adaptations as necessary.

The Weekly Assignment Sheet is completed by the general education teacher on a weekly basis (see Figure 4.4). Teachers use this form to communicate events, such as tests, assignments, projects, and other activities. In this way, teachers provide materials in advance that need to be modified. They attach copies of the original test or assignment to the

Infused skills grid

Student: _Romielle_
Age and grade: _12/eighth_
Completed by: _Mrs. Day_
Date: _11/17/00_

Daily schedule

Daily schedule	Self-care— dressing	Social— Initiate interactions	Communication "w" questions	Communication "wants and needs"	Personal responsibility (arrive on time)
Arrival/departure		X	X	X	X
Humanities		X	X	X	X
Math		X	X	X	X
Physical education	X	X	X	X	X
Lunch		X	X	X	
Science		X	X	X	X
Elective rotation		X	X	X	X
Mark here if the infused skill has been identified by →					
Family	X				
Student			X	X	
Peers		X		X	X
School		X	X		X

Figure 4.2. The infused skills grid shows how functional skills can be infused into the daily routine of the student.

56

Science

Major Unit Objectives

- Students will understand the structure and function of the cell.
- Students will identify the parts of the cell.
- Students will identify how cells are organized in multicellular organisms.

Materials

1. Book: *Modern Biology*
2. Educational videotapes related to chapter contents
3. Art supplies for cell projects
4. Chapter worksheets
5. Primary source: *Science* magazine article on the cell
6. University biology professor to discuss current research on cells

   Modifications

   1. Book chapters read and recorded on audiotape
   4. Worksheets modified to emphasize key points of chapters

Instructional Arrangements

1. Large-group instruction with overheads to introduce the cell
2. Small groups to complete labs, worksheets, mind maps, and chapter review
3. Two cell labs to be completed with partners (using onion skin and Jell-O)
4. Individual time to complete illustrated vocabulary

   Modifications

   1. Copy of the teacher's overhead transparencies given to student with disabilities
   1. One peer takes notes in class; another student types notes on the computer for each of them
   2. Use of "Read, write, pair, share" strategy for a chapter review

Projects

1. Homework: Complete vocabulary and bring in Jell-O food items
2. "Design a cell" and "Parts of the cell" group projects and presentations
3. Write-up for each completed lab with illustrations

   Modifications

   1. Magazine pictures to illustrate key points
   3. Lab write-up sheet completed by a peer using a computer; supplemental illustrations write-up

Assessments

1. Illustrated vocabulary words added to the class portfolio.
2. Culminating activity: "Design a cell" and "Parts of the cell" projects
3. Chapter test

   Modifications

   3. Chapter test read orally with additional time given, reducing the number of options for multiple choice questions and providing options for short answer questions

Figure 4.3. Sample unit lesson plan in the subject of science.

ASSIGNMENTS

WEEK OF: 10 / 6

Teacher's name: _Mr. Lee_

Student's name: _Romielle_

	Tests	Worksheets	Projects	Other
Monday		X		X

Read aloud Chapter 1 of Number the Stars (NS)
Partner read Chapter 2
Lecture on causes of WWII

	Tests	Worksheets	Projects	Other
Tuesday		X	X	X

Quick write on NS
Read loud Chapter 3
Partner read Chapter 4
Concept maps of book thus far

	Tests	Worksheets	Projects	Other
Wednesday	X	X	X	X

Info. quiz on NS book
Read aloud Chapter 5
Partner read Chapter 6
Film—WWII

	Tests	Worksheets	Projects	Other
Thursday			X	X

Reaction posters on WWII
Read aloud Chapter 7
Partner read Chapter 8
Lecture on course of WWII

	Tests	Worksheets	Projects	Other
Friday			X	

Presentations on final project proposal
Notebook checks

Comments: _Make sure groups are meeting to develop their final proposal._

Please return this form to _____Ms. Frey's_____ box. Thanks!

Figure 4.4. The weekly assignment sheet is used to communicate events, such as tests, assignments, and projects.

form, and the inclusion support teacher makes the necessary modifications.

Access to interesting, relevant, and challenging core curriculum is key to the success that students experience in middle school. As teachers design curriculum, they must also ensure that all students can gain access to the curriculum through instructional strategies (which are discussed in the next chapter), accommodations, and modifications. The recommendations and strategies outlined in the remainder of this book require us to assume that all students have access to this most engaging core curriculum.

"Things don't just happen. They are made to happen." —*John F. Kennedy*

5

Differentiated Instruction for Diverse Middle School Students

Douglas Fisher
Craig H. Kennedy

Megumi and Cory are both students in Ms. Robinson's seventh-grade humanities class. Megumi and Cory have known each other since elementary school. They play at each other's houses, study together, sit together in class, and read together. They especially like books that are about science and solving mysteries. Megumi doesn't say much but makes choices with her eyes and communicates with an electronic speech output device. This assistive technology, as well as the curriculum adaptations and modifications that are provided by the special educator, ensure Megumi's success in the humanities class. They allow Megumi to participate in reading through the use of her augmentative communication system. For example, Megumi's teacher may highlight one sentence from a paragraph and ask Megumi to respond using her speech output device. While Megumi has an identified cognitive disability, Cory does not. Their friendship started years ago when Megumi moved into the neighborhood. Megumi loves to perform, whereas Cory is rather shy. They were in their first school play together in fourth grade.

Ms. Robinson has books everywhere in her classroom. They are in the readers' corner, throughout the computer center, in the classroom library, and all throughout her desk. Ms. Robinson knows the richness of literature and how it illuminates the lives of children, parents, and teachers. She knows that books can open the minds and hearts of readers through humor, colorful illustrations, and imaginative ideas. Ms. Robinson says, "Students must encounter a reading program that contains high-quality literature organized around central issues, including themes of tolerance and differences."

Looking inside Ms. Robinson's classroom will reveal the strategies that she uses with her students. She encourages families to use the strategies to reinforce her literacy efforts at school. In addition, Ms. Robinson differentiates her instruction for the broad range of learner abilities in her classroom. Many of the strategies in this chapter are used at home and at school or have implications for both learning environments. These strategies include read alouds, visits to the library, selecting appropriate books, dedicated reading time, using alternative text formats, and performing as a way to learn.

READ ALOUDS

Current research supports what parents have always known—reading aloud to children benefits their language development and acquisition of positive social skills and strengthens the parent–child bond. Even infants who are not yet able to process the content of what is being read and sung to them thrive on the physical contact and richness of language that comes through a read aloud. Ms. Robinson reads to her students every day during class. She has found that children who have difficulty maintaining attention for long periods of time enjoy read alouds that are broken down into smaller segments. Ms. Robinson varies her selections for read alouds. Sometimes she reads narratives, whereas at other times she reads the newspaper, magazines, a social studies textbook, or nonnarrative books. She typically selects books that are just a little more difficult than the books that students can read on their own.

VISITS TO THE LIBRARY

Regular visits to the local public library provide children with access to a variety of books, videos, music, and audiotapes. Many of the students in Ms. Robinson's class do not have many books at home, so library visits are an effective way to ensure that students have appropriate reading materials. Ms. Robinson believes that every student in her class should own and use a public library card. She also believes that family trips to the library convey the important message that reading is a valued activity in the family. Also, it serves as an inexpensive outing for all members of the family to share and enjoy.

In addition to the time that children spend in the public library with and without their families, students in Ms. Robinson's class visit the school library to check out books at least once each week. They also have access to a number of books in their classroom library. Students have multiple opportunities to borrow the books and read them at home with their families.

SELECTING APPROPRIATE BOOKS

Readers love stories that contain characters who resemble themselves. Children with disabilities, like Megumi, are not any different. Along with classics and other favorites, Ms. Robinson recommends stories that focus on diversity, including differences in communication styles and abilities. These types of books give a voice to all children. Ms. Robinson warns parents and teachers to be critical consumers of the books that they select. Disability literature should meet the criteria set for all books: well written with fully developed characters involved in engaging and entertaining story lines. A poorly written book that contains a character with a disability should always be rejected.

Ms. Robinson believes that there are three criteria for selecting books. First, books should be challenging but not frustrating for students. Therefore, her classroom contains books with a wide range of difficulty levels. This is especially helpful for students with cognitive disabilities and those who are less fluent in English. Second, Ms. Robinson's classroom is filled with books that have received national awards, including the National Book Award and Newbery Award (local bookstores have lists of these books). Third, Ms. Robinson believes that the book collection must be multicultural. Her classroom is filled with books about a variety of people. She added to her classroom library a number of titles about people with disabilities when she learned that Megumi was going to be joining her class.

DEDICATED READING TIME

Dedicated reading time sets for children a positive example about the importance and value that the adults in their lives place on literacy. Ms.

Robinson recommends that each family member select his or her own materials to be read during this designated time. Mitchel, another student in Ms. Robinson's class, reads with his family on Monday, Wednesday, and Friday evenings. Some families choose other relaxing settings for this enjoyable activity, such as weekend visits to a local coffeehouse, a shady park, or the backyard patio. Cory's family reads in the backyard several times a week and at the park every weekend.

Ms. Robinson also dedicates time in her class everyday for reading. She calls this time independent reading. During this time, the students select a book that interests them and find a place to read. Some students read at their desks; others read on the floor, on beanbags, or in the classroom library. Regardless of where they read, everyone, including the teacher, reads a book for the entire 20-minute period.

USING ALTERNATIVE TEXT FORMATS

Ms. Robinson often reminds parents that less fluent readers and students who are auditory learners can enjoy books on tape or CD, picture books, or the comics section from the Sunday newspaper. The growing popularity of listening to audio recordings of books has led to a boom in the availability of a wide variety of bestsellers and classics. It is an enjoyable way to ."read" books for children who may not currently have the skills to read independently. Ms. Robinson recommends that families who spend time in the car should choose a book for active listening. She also notes that parents can assist children in the comprehension of the story and its characters by asking several questions about the story.

Videos of books and stories often are overlooked as tools for reading. As Ms. Robinson says, "Visual literacy is increasingly recognized as an important skill in today's multimedia society." Techniques for increasing visual literacy skills include reading a book first, then viewing the video version of the same book. After viewing the video, a discussion about the similarities and differences between the two is an especially helpful comprehension aide for many students. Ms. Robinson always informs parents of the books that her class is reading. When there is a video available, she encourages parents to borrow it from the classroom library. When Ms. Robinson shows a video, she stops it from time to time and asks questions concerning comprehension (What just happened? Why did the boy choose to do that?) and prediction (What do you think will happen next?). She always invites families in for video days. These same questions can be used at home to expand the readers' understanding. A child's familiarity with these questions will serve them well in their literacy acquisition.

Performing as a Way to Learn

Ms. Robinson and the students in her class love to perform the stories that they are reading. Ms. Robinson knows that comprehension for all students is enhanced when she uses drama, music, and movement. Children who struggle with concepts of character development, sequence, and motivation can experience stories in other ways when performance techniques are used. For example, Ms. Robinson often uses a reader's theater strategy in which Megumi and Cory may assume the roles of characters and re-create the dialogue from the text. Viewers follow along in the text to reinforce their own skills. While Cory uses her voice to play her part, Megumi uses her electronic voice output device. Megumi's parents and support staff help her prepare for her role in the reader's theater by programming the voice output device the night before the performance and by helping her rehearse her lines. Cory's family also helps her prepare for her role the night before by helping her rehearse the lines she will recite and providing her with feedback about her acting.

In addition to the time that students perform at school, many of the students in Ms. Robinson's class are involved in community theater and after-school programs. These additional opportunities are selected by families for their reinforcement of the ideas that students learn at school. Cory and Megumi both attend a community theater program sponsored by the local Boys and Girls Club. Their families take turns driving, and everyone loves the performances that are scheduled every other week.

Differentiating Instruction

In addition to the reading strategies that Ms. Robinson uses in her class, she has a number of differentiated instructional strategies available for her use (Rutherford, 1998; Tomlinson, 1995). Although Ms. Robinson uses her literacy strategies every day, she uses various differentiated instructional strategies based on specific lessons. She does not use all of these strategies every day.

Compacting

In compacting, students are assessed on their prior knowledge. Students who already know the material are assigned other tasks, such as peer tutoring, library research, math labs, and so forth. This allows Ms. Robinson to focus her lesson on the students who really need the extra knowledge. Two rules guide her use of this strategy. First, the pre-assessment changes every week. One week it could be paper and pencil, the next week it could be small groups, the next week it could be oral, and the following week it could be a performance. Second, all students must take the final assessment of the material, and their grade is based on that score. In addition to creating an in-class tutoring system, Ms. Robinson has noticed that some of the students who were eligible for compacting out decided not to because they learned that they did better on the tests when they participated in the lesson. Ms. Robinson found this to be an effective way to engage some of her students in the learning process. However, it should be noted that not all students may benefit from this strategy.

Independent Projects

Ms. Robinson believes that work done outside school should be interesting and should require students to work with at least one other person. She is most interested in independent projects (previously called homework) that require students to interact with their families. She is least interested in independent projects that encourage students to sit in their bedrooms by themselves. Ms. Robinson also likes independent projects that are challenging for students but not frustrating. This has led her to develop several projects so that all of her students are not doing the same project each night. For example, prior to a discussion of World War II, Ms. Robinson asked 11 students to interview their parents and their grandparents about life during the 1940s, 10 students worked in pairs to collect pictures and videos from the period before the war, and 12 students produced a 3-minute video about poverty during the war.

Interest Groups

Ms. Robinson's school has an advisory period because only half of the students in the school are at lunch at one time. To provide educational opportunities for the students who are not at lunch, Ms. Robinson, along with other teachers, offers advisory classes. During these classes, students will have the opportunity to choose research topics. For example, Ms. Robinson has offered such diverse topics as the Titanic, 3-D art, horror novels, and careers in human services. These advisory interest groups, which last for 3 weeks, are full of students who are interested in a specific topic. At the end of the 3 weeks, students get to pick a new topic. Some students pick Ms. Robinson regardless of what topic she is covering; others make different choices each session. Ms. Robinson believes that these interest groups allow students to experience the richness of a curriculum and make choices about what they want to learn. She also knows that the time she spends in advisory classes allows her to get to know students well.

Concept Maps and Character Webs

Visual representations of complex ideas help students organize information. Developing concept or semantic maps is one strategy used by teachers because it provides insights on students' knowledge about the topic. Typically, the main idea is placed in the center of the paper with a small circle drawn around it. Then, lines are drawn from the circle to the ideas that connect with the main idea. As you can imagine, there can be several subideas to a main idea, and each subidea can have several branches of ideas. For example, Ms. Robinson's class was studying ancient civilizations. One day she asked each student to take out a piece of paper and write the words "Greek life" inside a small circle. The students then were asked to brainstorm for ideas that were connected to their main idea. Following this brainstorming session, students were asked to transform their concept map into a three-paragraph paper. Ms. Robinson also uses concept maps, arranged in groups of four, as a way to review for tests. Not only can her students review information this way, but she can gain insights about areas that students may not understand.

Ms. Robinson uses character webs to focus her students' thinking on people. When the class was reading *Hatchet* (Paulsen, 1987), each student was given a simple drawing of a person's head. As they learned more about Brian (the main character in the book), the students illustrated the simple drawing and placed key words around the head to describe him. Ms. Robinson has found that the character webs help all of her students understand character development. She was especially pleased to find that her students with learning disabilities significantly improved their understanding of the story when they were required to create character webs. In addition to concept maps, Ms. Robinson uses art, illustrated vocabulary, videos, and web sites to assist students in creating visual representations.

Writing Prompts and Questions

Ms. Robinson works with students to create a series of questions to answer as they read the text. She has found that this helps them focus on specific information while they are reading. This may be as simple as having students read the questions before, after, and throughout the reading of the chapter. Focusing on the questions helps students chunk, summarize, and synthesize the newly acquired information. When there are no questions at the end of the unit, Ms. Robinson and her students create questions on which they can focus during their reading. These questions often are developed during the "what I want to learn" part of the KWL (What do you KNOW, what do you WANT to know, and what did you LEARN) (Ogle, 1986, 1996) or by changing text subheadings into questions.

However, during writing assignments, Ms. Robinson has found that students perform better when she changes the questions into sentence starters. For example, instead of asking students to respond to the question, "When Brian was stranded on the island, how did he survive?" Ms. Robinson provides students several sentence starters, including, "Brian lived on an island by . . ." "In addition to fish that Brian caught to eat, he . . ." and, "Brian found shelter . . ."

Tiered Assignments and Tests

Ms. Robinson has found that when students have choices in their assignments, they perform better. For this reason, she has a full page of assignments that students can complete for her class. Each assignment is worth a maximum number of points, and students select which assignments to complete based on their interests. Although other teachers have different rules regarding tiered assignments, Ms. Robinson lets her students do as many assignments as they want to earn the grade that they want in her class.

In addition to tiered assignments, Ms. Robinson uses tiered tests. Her unit tests have five parts: true and false, multiple choice, short answer, short essay with illustration, and long essay. Ms. Robinson likes her students to experience different ways of demonstrating their knowledge so that they will do well on the statewide assessments. Her use of tiered tests is somewhat unique. During test time, students are required to complete two sections of the test. When she returns the test the following day, she has graded the two sections that each student completed. The students then complete one more section of the test. She does this for several reasons. First, students can demonstrate their knowledge the best way they know how. Second, students learn to use the test as a tool. That is, students are able to apply their correct answers to questions on subsequent tests. Third, students talk about the test during passing periods and lunch after the first administration. Whereas the students think they are being sly, Ms. Robinson likes that they are using their time to talk about the curriculum. Finally, Ms. Robinson likes that these tests communicate to the students that knowledge is never complete, that there is always more to know and learn.

FLEXIBLE GROUPING

Classroom instruction in the United States has been traditionally characterized by permanent homogeneous ability groups constituted by teacher assessment of student achievement. Research conducted during the past two decades has indicated that permanent ability grouping can create serious social and emotional problems for students. As a result, Ms. Robinson is attempting to implement more flexible grouping patterns that accommodate the interplay of ideas among her students. She believes that teachers should feel comfortable using many types of grouping patterns for many different purposes. For example, whole-class instruction is useful when she has short bits of information to convey to students, such as the causes of World War II, or when reinforcing a skill or strategy. She also knows that there are other effective ways to group students. In addition to whole-class homogeneous grouping, Ms. Robinson uses flexible grouping patterns to meet the needs of her increasingly diverse student population. Grouping patterns that are flexible provide teachers with an opportunity to observe students working in a variety of situations, including working alone, working with partners, and working in small, cooperative teams.

Ms. Robinson believes that students should experience three types of groups per week: teacher-selected groups, student-selected groups, and random groups. During teacher-selected group time, Ms. Robinson uses the Center Activity Rotation System (CARS; Lapp, Fisher, & Flood, 1999). Within this rotation system, students are divided into heterogeneous cooperative groups. Each of the groups works at a learning center that is related to the theme that the whole class is studying. In addition to the heterogeneous groups, Ms. Robinson works with specific students at a teacher center. Each day, she selects specific students to work with her in a small teacher group. They will discuss a specific skill, or Ms. Robinson will teach explicitly and directly about a specific piece of information. To ensure that all students receive small-group instruction, Ms. Robinson meets with each student during center rotations. Here are a few of the centers that Ms. Robinson uses to teach her students about the Civil War.

One center involves fraction quilts. This center requires students to apply their math knowledge and re-create quilts similar to those made by slaves during Civil War times. Another center focuses on writing. At this center, students begin their biographies. Students understand the task because the whole class has been reading biographies about people who lived during Civil War times. At a third center, students view a film about life during the Civil War. Ms. Robinson wants to ensure that her students have a visual understanding of the life and times of American history. She also wants to ensure that her students who are less fluent in English have a visual representation of the vocabulary that the class is discussing. At the next center, students meet to discuss the text that the whole class is reading. They also record their responses and predictions to share during the teacher read aloud. At another center, students read independently from narrative and nonnarrative books. This center reinforces the importance of reading and supplements the free-choice reading that students do daily. A teacher center is involved in all of Ms. Robinson's lessons using CARS. Ms. Robinson meets with different groups each day. This allows her to address specific skills and needs to assess her students' learning progress.

In addition to these teacher-selected groups, Ms. Robinson designs lessons in which students select their own groups. This often happens during independent projects or library research. Finally, Ms. Robinson uses random groups to ensure that students have the opportunity to interact with everyone in the class. Her favorite way of interacting is with playing cards. Each student gets a card, and then all of the students with the same number meet. This strategy also allows for a natural regroup when the students gather in groups of diamonds, hearts, spades, and clubs. For additional information about grouping, see Lapp et al. (1999) or Reutzel (1999).

Many of the supports that students with disabilities require can be provided as part of the instructional arrangements in the general education classroom. Several years of research suggest that these instructional strategies are beneficial for all students, not only those with disabilities (Gambrell, Morrow, Neuman, & Pressley, 1999; McGregor & Vogelsberg, 1998; Tomlinson, 1995). Taken together, curriculum and instruction supports address many of the support needs for students with disabilities. Chapter 6 addresses assessment strategies that are useful in demonstrating what students have learned and their achievement.

Appendix

DIFFERENTIATED INSTRUCTION RESOURCES

Differentiating instruction for advanced learners in the mixed-ability middle school classroom. ERIC Digest E536. Available www.ed.gov/databases/ERIC_Digests/ed389141.html

Moon, T., Tomlinson, C., & Callahan, C. (1997). *Academic diversity in the middle school: Results of a national survey of middle school administrators and teachers* (Research Monograph 95124). Storrs, CT: National Research Center on the Gifted and Talented.

Technology and differentiated instruction web resources. Available k12.albemarle.org/Technology/DI

Tomlinson, C. (1995). *How to differentiate instruction in the mixed ability classroom.* Alexandria, VA: Association for Supervision and Curriculum Development.

Tomlinson, C. (1996). *Differentiating instruction for mixed-ability classrooms: A professional inquiry kit.* Alexandria, VA: Association for Supervision and Curriculum Development.

Tomlinson, C. (1997). *Differentiating instruction: A video staff development package.* Alexandria, VA: Association for Supervision and Curriculum Development.

Tomlinson, C. (1998). Curriculum and instruction for gifted learners in the middle grades: What would it take. In R. Williamson & H. Johnston (Eds.), *Able learners in the middle level school: Identifying talent and maximizing potential* (pp. 21–32). Reston, VA: National Association of Secondary School Principals.

Tomlinson, C. (1998). Differentiating instruction for gifted learners in mixed ability settings: Challenge and potential. In J.A. Leroux (Ed.), *Connecting the gifted community worldwide.* Seattle: Selected proceedings from the 12th World Conference of the World Council for Gifted and Talented Children.

Tomlinson, C. (1999). *The differentiated classroom: Responding to the needs of all learners.* Alexandria, VA: Association for Supervision and Curriculum Development.

Tomlinson, C., & Allan, S. (in press). *Providing leadership for differentiated schools and classrooms.* Alexandria, VA: Association for Supervision and Curriculum Development.

Willis, S., & Winter, L.M. (2000). *Differentiating instruction: Finding manageable ways to meet individual needs* (excerpt). Available www.ascd.org/readingroom/cupdate/2000/1win.html

"Disorder is simply a harmony to which many are unaccustomed." —John Cage

6

Linking Assessment to Accountability and Instruction

Douglas Fisher
Craig H. Kennedy

Assessment has always been, and likely always will be, a major component of schooling. Now more than ever before, educators are inundated with choices as they select assessments that will provide appropriate information about students' strengths and needs. Selecting assessments has proved especially challenging for teachers of students with disabilities (National Center for Educational Outcomes, 1994). Assessment tools range from informal teacher-designed measures to standardized tests (see Table 6.1 for an overview of types of assessments). Teachers often use assessments to monitor student outcomes and to better understand day-to-day changes in student performance. Statewide assessments often are used for accountability purposes for ranking student, teacher, school, and district performance. However, the ultimate goal of assessment is improved student outcomes. The guiding principle of this chapter is that assessment systems, especially those used

Table 6.1.   Formal and informal assessments

Type	Purpose	Procedure
Formal Assessment		
Standardized tests	To measure a student's performance in a variety of skills and compare those scores with those of students in other geographic locations	Administer at set intervals; students answer questions from booklet on standard forms
Criterion-referenced tests	To indicate attainment of mastery on specific instructional objectives, usually by answering a percentage of questions correctly	Administer with lesson plans; students read items and answer on separate paper
Informal Assessment		
Observations	To assess a student's use of language in a variety of instructional settings	Observe and record student's use of language, often written in logs or journals
Skills checklists	To track a student's development by noting which skills have become or are becoming part of a repertoire	Set up a checklist of desirable skills in language arts and periodically observe the student to determine which have been attained
Portfolio assessment	To document in a variety of ways how a student has developed as a language user	Collect samples of the student's work, including published writing, taped oral readings, and conference notes
Conferencing	To provide opportunities for the teacher and student to discuss development	Meet at set times to review performance and discuss instruction that may be required for student to progress

Table 6.1.   (*continued*)

Peer reviews	To involve students in the evaluation process and to build their evaluative and interactive skills	Give students guidelines for evaluation; two or more meet to discuss each other's work; peer's grade is factored into final grade
Self-assessment	To empower students by making them responsible for and reflective of their own work	Evaluate performance and progress via checklists, interactions, inventories, conferences, and portfolios

Adapted from Flood, Lapp, & Wood, 1997. *Staff development guide.* New York: Macmillan/McGraw-Hill; adapted by permission.

for accountability, should encourage the involvement of all students, including those with disabilities, and focus on improving academic and social development. The first section of this chapter focuses on statewide assessments used for accountability and the ways that students with disabilities participate in them. The second section of this chapter focuses on classroom assessments used to illustrate instructional practices and provides examples of how students with and without disabilities benefit from linking assessments to instruction.

WHY ASSESS STUDENTS?

As the public continues to demand increased accountability from schools and as school administrators and policymakers increase their use of performance and outcome data for decision making, people are paying more attention to who gets tested, what kinds of tests are used, and what the results mean. It is important to understand that students can be assessed for a wide variety of purposes:

- Identifying student performance characteristics (e.g., assessing developmental status, monitoring and communicating student progress, certifying competency)
- Improving instruction and student performance (e.g., evaluating instructional outcomes, modifying instructional strategies, identifying instructional needs)
- Evaluating program effectiveness
- Providing information for school system accountability

Also, it is important to understand that there are multiple types of tests within one state or district assessment system. For example, state assessments vary on the following characteristics: 1) the subject areas and grade levels tested, 2) the item formats used, and 3) the types of skills tested (e.g., basic versus higher order thinking skills). In addition, depending on the purpose of the test, results can be reported on several different levels, including student, classroom, grade, school, district, state, and national. Although it is important to keep in mind the different purposes and levels of assessment in education, this chapter focuses primarily on the inclusion of students with disabilities within assessment systems.

WHAT IS THE RELATIONSHIP BETWEEN STANDARDS AND ASSESSMENT?

The proponents of standards-based systemic reform maintain that if high, rigorous standards are created for all students and are clearly communicated to educators, students, family members, business leaders, policymakers, and the community at large, then a coordinated effort can be mounted to focus on increased achievement (NASBE, 1996). The outcome is intended to raise expectations for all students—those who are from impoverished homes, those with limited English proficiency, and those with disabilities that will result in improved performance and achievement. In other words, the bar is raised for all students and the entire system is focused on helping them achieve higher expectations.

Student assessment, then, becomes the process by which these standards are measured. However, many current assessment systems are not aligned with district or state standards. In addition, some states use only standardized, multiple-choice tests that cannot be given to those who speak English as a second language or those with disabilities. As a result, many students are excluded from testing and accountability systems. The result is assessment data that do not reflect the actual student population and may or may not provide useful information about how students attain the standards.

HOW CAN THE PARTICIPATION OF STUDENTS WITH DISABILITIES IN STATEWIDE ASSESSMENT SYSTEMS BE INCREASED?

As with many educational policies, there is a great deal of variation among states regarding the inclusion of students with disabilities in statewide assessments. In many states, assessment reform is an integral part of standards-based reform. These reforms focus on developing statewide tests that are aligned with the state content and performance standards. For example, in Tennessee, the standards, curriculum, assessment, and reporting system has been aligned. Similarly, in Kentucky, assessment systems in which all students participate have been created (Kleinert et al., 1997). However, there has been considerable variation in how states are implementing these new statewide assessments, the status of the process, and the consequences of the results. In an effort to allow people from different states to communicate about and evaluate their systems, a number of key questions have been developed, including the following (Fisher, Roach, & Kearns, 1998):

- Does the state have written guidelines and exemplars for the participation of students with disabilities in state assessments used for accountability purposes?
- Does the state have written guidelines and exemplars for the use of accommodations by students with disabilities in state assessment systems?
- Does the state prohibit students from being excluded from the state assessment system based on disability?
- Does the state have written guidelines and exemplars for reporting results for students with disabilities in state assessments?

Students with disabilities can participate in a statewide assessment process in one of three ways. First, a student may participate like any other student in a traditional standardized assessment. Second, a student may participate through the use of specially designed accommodations that are both specified on a student's IEP *and* used routinely during the instruction for that student (see Table 6.2 for a sample of accommodations used in statewide assessment systems). Third, a student may participate through an alternative assessment. Alternative assessments are designed to accommodate students with disabilities for whom writing and mathematics tests, performance events, and traditional assessments would be inappropriate (Kleinert et al., 1997).

An example of how alternative assessment systems work can be taken from Tennessee. The Tennessee system focuses on assessing the extent to which students with significant disabilities receive instructional practices that have been empirically demonstrated to provide learning benefits. On a yearly basis, teachers of students with significant disabilities must submit information that demonstrates the degree to which each of their students has received these best practices and how the students have benefited. This provides a high degree of accountability regarding the quality of instruction that students receive and that can be evaluated at the student, teacher, school, and local education agency levels.

Table 6.2. Accommodations for standardized achievement testing

Flexible scheduling	Flexible setting	Revised test format	Revised test directions	Use of aids to interpret test items	Use of aids to respond to test items
time extension	individual administration	braille editions or transcriptions	rewriting or reformatting directions	special equipment	equipment to record responses
testing duration	small-group administration	large-print transcriptions or other transcriptions	emphasizing key words in directions	proctor assistance/readers: repeat oral comprehension items more than specified in directions; read or sign test passages, questions, items, and multiple-choice responses; provide cues to maintain on task behavior	scribes
successive administrations	adaptive or special equipment at regular testing location	changes in presentation of test items	reading standard directions		computational aids—calculators or arithmetic tables
multiple days	adaptive or special equipment at separate location	changes in space for answers			

The accommodations may involve 1) the way in which test items are presented to students, 2) the student's methods of responding to test items, or 3) the process that a student uses to derive responses to test items.

Although statewide assessments are gaining increased attention, especially in the media, classroom assessments are equally important. Teachers use classroom assessments to plan and evaluate their instruction. Ultimately, these classroom assessments and the planning that results should have an impact on the statewide assessments noted previously.

HOW DO TEACHERS USE
ASSESSMENTS TO PLAN INSTRUCTION?

The primary use of assessment information for teachers is to make instructional decisions that produce improved student performance and learning. For example, Mr. Escobar uses a speaking checklist (see Figure 6.1) to ensure that his students have ample opportunity to develop oral literacy skills in his eighth-grade science class. Recently, Mr. Escobar noticed that Jamie, a student in his first-period class who was identified as having a learning disability, was not delineating minor points that supported her primary thesis during her oral presentation. When asked to provide an impromptu speech on food digestion, Jamie stood and said, "Food is digested in the stomach. The stomach does the work." While the students were working on their assignments that day, Mr. Escobar was able to provide explicit instruction to Jamie as they reread the chapter together. Mr. Escobar helped Jamie realize the need for a logical flow of ideas and to support one's ideas to make a point. At the end of the period, Jamie stood and presented the following: "Digestion begins with chewing and continues in the stomach when acids combine with the food. The entire process takes several hours and continues through the intestines."

Mr. Escobar also uses a holistic writing rubric to assess his students. When teachers use this type of assessment system, they examine the total writing product, not a group of separate parts. These scores are based on guides, called rubrics, which are the criteria against which each piece of writing is evaluated. Teachers can choose from among an eight-point, a six-point, and a four-point scoring scale (see Table 6.3). Mr. Escobar uses rubrics with even numbers to avoid an average score. He believes that average provides little information for the teacher or the student. Neither one has a clear idea whether the guidelines were addressed adequately or inadequately. The choice of the rubric scoring system depends on the teacher's objective for the assessment of student performance. The eight-point scale offers the most flexibility and finest distinction in quality. The six-point scale also offers a range of scores with less variation. The four-point scale is used to make broader evaluations of writing and easily becomes a pass-or-fail evaluation of a paper.

Name: _____

When _____ speaks in a group, he/she:
           (name)

	Sept.	Dec.	March	June
Sticks to the topic				
Builds support for the subject				
Speaks clearly				
Takes turns and waits to talk				
Talks so others in the group can hear				
Speaks smoothly				
Uses courteous language				
Presents in an organized and interesting way				
Supports the topical thesis				
Answers questions effectively				
Is comfortable speaking publicly				
Maintains listeners' interest				
Volunteers to answer in class				
Speaks only to those who share the same lesson plan				

Figure 6.1.   The speaking checklist is used to track a student's skills.

When James, a student with a significant cognitive disability, submitted his paper, Mr. Escobar used the eight-point scale. James's paper was done with pictures selected from magazines, based on the accommodations and modifications outlined in his IEP. Mr. Escobar looked for organization, creativity, content, and style when evaluating James's paper. He was impressed that James had created visual representations of the beginning, middle, and end of the novel *The Giver* (Lowry, 1993). Mr. Escobar gave James a 7 on his paper because he realized that although James clearly demonstrated his creativity in his visual essay, he missed a key point of the content—what is truth.

Mr. Escobar also uses cloze assessments to ensure that the reading material he selects is challenging but not frustrating for his students. Cloze is one type of measurement of comprehension or readability in which a reading selection is given and certain words are deleted. The student must then provide closure by inserting the proper words according

Table 6.3. Holistic writing rubrics

Eight-point scale	Six-point scale	Four-point scale
8 Excellent paper. A 9 is reserved for papers that are nearly perfect in content, organization, mechanics, and language use. Both 8 and 9 are excellent papers in areas of form and content, with 9s representing higher quality.	**6–5** Excellent paper. A 6 is reserved for papers that are nearly perfect in content, organization, mechanics, and language use. Both 5 and 6 are excellent papers in areas of form and content, with 6s representing higher quality.	**4** An excellent paper that is well organized and displays facile use of language, content, and mechanics.
7 Still an excellent paper, but not quite as organized, creative, and articulate as an 8 paper.	**4** A passing paper judged adequate in terms of content, organization, mechanics, and style. It may lack imagination and creativity.	**3** A paper that demonstrates adequate organization, content, language use, and handling of mechanics. It may lack imagination and creativity.
6–5 An adequate paper but deficient in its organization, use of content, style, or mechanics.	**3** A lower-half paper that is weak in content, organization, style, or mechanics.	**2** A lower-half paper that is weak in content, organization, style, or mechanics.
4–3 A lower-half paper that is weak in content, organization, style, or mechanics.	**2** A very weak paper that addresses the topic but is loosely organized, with serious faults in organization, content, language use, style, or mechanics.	**1** An unacceptable paper that addresses the topic but is weak in organization, content, or language use and is full of errors in mechanics.
2 A very weak paper that addresses the topic but is loosely organized, with serious faults in organization, content, language use, style, or mechanics.	**1** A paper that addresses the topic but is disorganized, inarticulate, and full of errors.	
1 A paper that addresses the topic but is disorganized, inarticulate, and full of errors.		

to context clues. Students with disabilities may do this orally, in writing, with eye gaze, with pictures, or with assistance from peers. This informal, criterion-referenced assessment procedure is useful for teachers for two reasons. First, it is flexible enough to allow teachers to assess large groups of students at the same time or individually assess students. Second, the information gathered in the assessment procedure can be used to select for students reading material that is challenging but not frustrating. The procedure includes the following guidelines:

1. Select a student text of approximately 250 words. The passage should be in the language that the teacher wishes to assess.
2. Even if a 250-word passage ends in the middle of a sentence, use only the 250 words (see Figure 6.2).
3. Delete every fifth word and insert a straight line in place of each missing word.
4. The passage should contain approximately 50 straight lines after deletions have been made (see Figure 6.2).
5. If a teacher is unsure of text difficulty, he or she can select twelve 250-word passages that are approximately eight pages apart. This wide range of passages will ensure a representative sample of text difficulty. If a teacher has previously selected a passage that represents difficulty, he or she should administer it.
6. Give every student all of the passages.
7. Students are asked to insert the missing words. No time limits are set.
8. Responses are correct even if misspelled.
9. Each correct closure is worth two points.
10. Score the assessment as follows: 58–100 points indicates an *independent* reading level for the student, 44–57 points indicates that this is the *instructional* level for the student, and less than 44 points indicates that the material is in the student's *frustration* level.

Once the results are tallied, teachers have a general idea of where to begin instruction in this or a similar text. By studying the type of errors that students make, teachers can make decisions about future reading instruction. Although many educators may suggest that the exact word must be inserted, it is acceptable for the inserted word to be counted as correct if it is the appropriate part of speech and does not alter the text meaning. The child's performance, rather than the score, is the key to this successful integration of assessment and instruction. As the students' responses are analyzed, it is important to determine how the students understand the passage. This type of scrutiny can help with planning appropriate instruction.

She began to describe this year's group and its variety of personalities, though she singled no one out by name. She mentioned that there was one who had singular skills at caretaking, another who loved new children, one with unusual scientific aptitude, and a fourth for whom physical labor was an obvious pleasure. Jonas shifted in his seat, trying to recognize each reference as one of his groupmates. The caretaking skills were no doubt those of Fiona, on his left; he remembered noticing the tenderness with which she had bathed the old [and so forth to 250 words].

She began to describe _____ year's group and its _____ of personalities, though she _____ no one out by _____. She mentioned that there _____ one who had singular _____ at caretaking, another who _____ new children, one with unusual _____ aptitude, and a fourth _____ whom physical labor was _____ obvious pleasure. Jonas shifted _____ his seat, trying to _____ each reference as one _____ his groupmates. The caretaking _____ were no doubt those _____ Fiona, on his left; _____ remembered noticing the tenderness _____ which she had bathed the old [and so forth to 250 words].

Figure 6.2.   Cloze assessments are used to measure readability and comprehension when a reading selection is given and certain words are deleted.

Another informal way that Mr. Escobar collects information about students involves the students' reflections on their own habits. This assessment is useful in determining instructional priorities and in providing the students the opportunity to develop self-assessment skills. Students should be encouraged to respond to specific questions about their learning and how they approach tasks. For example, they can write in a weekly journal, either alone or with a parent or a teacher. There are several possible considerations that students can be taught to use in self-evaluation (see Figure 6.3).

Teachers like Mr. Escobar tend to keep these assessment results in student portfolios as a demonstration of continued learning. Mr. Escobar uses a showcase portfolio in which students store a profile of themselves as a learner, samples of their work, and specific papers that he has used for assessment. These portfolios are shown frequently to families during conferences, back-to-school night, and IEP meetings.

Name: _____ Date: _____ Grade: _____

How am I doing at . . .

    Looking up words in the dictionary

    Rereading portions of the story to help my comprehension

    Writing a summary of the story

    Taking notes while reading

    Asking questions of teachers or friends to improve my comprehension

    Underlining words for recall

    Gaining comfort by speaking English

What type of help do I think I need?

Figure 6.3.   Self-evaluation sheet to be completed by the student.

As assessment results are shared with more and more people, teachers are presented with additional challenges. Fortunately, several recommendations exist to address these challenges (Beck, 1997). First, there are no inherently bad or good assessments. Assessments are useful only when teachers understand the purpose and use of the tool. For example, statewide achievement assessments are not likely to influence classroom instruction any more than classroom-based portfolios are likely to influence accountability systems. Both are useful, but each provides a different type of information.

Second, no one assessment provides sufficient information for all decision making. Teachers and administrators should use a variety of information sources for diagnosing students, for instructional planning, and for accountability. Useful assessments will confirm the information from other useful assessments. The more information a teacher has about students, the more confident he or she will be in developing lessons that match the students' current educational needs.

Teachers should take every assessment they plan to administer to students. Having answered the questions, performed the activities, or thought through the instructions ensures that the teacher is fully aware of the measures and how content is being assessed. The only way to gain an understanding of the dynamics of the assessment is to become a tested student.

With the advent of standards-based reform, states have increased the importance of student testing and accountability. Now, more than ever, it is important that all students be assessed and that their assessments be counted in building, district, and state accountability mechanisms.

Note: Figures 6.1, 6.3, and 9.1 are available for readers to download free of charge from the Brookes Publishing web site at www.brookespublishing.com/imsforms.

III

STUDENT SUPPORTS

"Unjustified isolation, we hold, is properly regarded as discrimination based on disability." —Justice Ruth Bader Ginsburg

7

Using Technology to Support Belonging and Achievement

Caren Sax

Instructional or educational technology (e.g., computers, CD-ROMs, multimedia equipment, the Internet) provides students with access to information presented in creative and interactive formats that enhance their ability to collect, analyze, and apply knowledge in useful ways. Government initiatives have supported these efforts by attempting to connect every school to the Internet and supporting the integration of technology throughout the curriculum (Fatemi, 1999; Thornburg, 1994). For the more than 5 million students with disabilities educated in public schools, access to these technologies and their benefits often requires the use of assistive technology equipment or devices. Assistive technology refers to any item, piece of equipment, or product system—whether acquired commercially, off the shelf, modified, or customized—that is used to increase, maintain, or improve functional capabilities of individuals with disabilities (Assistive Technology Act [ATA] of 1998, PL 105-394). Use of switches, computer hardware and software, mobility devices, communication systems, and low-tech adaptations enable students to gain access to the general education curriculum and increase their interaction with peers without disabilities (Sax et al., 1996). To participate in and respond to the general education curriculum, many students will use either or both of these technologies.

The number and variety of instructional and assistive technologies increased rapidly in the 1990s, expanding educational and social opportunities for students with disabilities. School districts that have become more proactive in designing and constructing barrier-free facilities (e.g., ramps, elevators, wide doors, lowered drinking fountains) must now institute fully accessible educational technology infrastructures. Legislation, including Section 508 of the Rehabilitation Act Amendments of 1992 (PL 102-569) and the ATA of 1998, has specified more guidelines that build on the efforts set forth by Section 504 of the Rehabilitation Act of 1973 (PL 93-112), the ADA of 1990, and IDEA of 1990 (PL 101-476), amended and reauthorized in 1997 (PL 105-17) with new regulations. This newer legislation mandates that school personnel consider accessibility issues prior to purchasing educational technology. To comply with these legal obligations and to prevent additional costs for retrofitting, consideration of accessibility in acquiring technology is a good idea. With significant appropriation of federal, state, and local dollars for educational technology, schools need to be aware of and avoid inadvertently creating barriers for students with disabilities.

The advances in instructional and assistive technology devices and equipment are linked to the efforts of the microchip and telecommunications industries as they attempt to meet the needs of an ever-expanding global society. New discoveries resulting from technology transfer efforts (e.g., transfer of materials and strategies from the defense industry) also contribute to the brisk pace of technological advances. The following examples include some of the major categories typically referred to as *assistive technology*. Because the products and companies change frequently, the following descriptions highlight the features commonly used by students with disabilities to succeed in school. A list of assistive technology web sites is included in the appendix at the end of this chapter to allow access to the latest styles and contact information. One must keep in mind that the use of assistive technology equipment and services is one of the considerations in designing support strategies for individual students. Teachers, families, and other professionals (e.g., speech-language therapists, occupational and physical therapists) also must consider an overall support plan that includes the use of curriculum modifications and personal supports (Castegnera et al., 1998).

COMPUTER ACCESS

A variety of adaptations in hardware and software has increased accessibility to computers for students with disabilities (Anson, 1997). For example, students who have visual impairments can use a large-print monitor and speech synthesizers to read printed text. Students who are blind can use a braille embosser and printer and a scanner to input text into the computer. To access the Internet, students use screen readers that vocalize the text on the screen of each web page. Specially designed software also supports multiple functions under one command. Some of these same accommodations can be useful for students with learning disabilities, such as the benefits of a screen-reading program for students who visually have difficulty processing information. For students who physically are unable to manipulate a keyboard in the standard manner, access is available through the use of a trackball or joystick, head pointer, sip-and-puff switch, ultrasonic pointer device, or software that enables the computer to respond to voice commands. Students who are deaf or who have hearing impairments benefit from the use of captions built into video and multimedia programs, as well as visual icons that replace sound cues on the computer. Many features are standard, allowing for universal access. Universal access tries to encourage attractive, marketable products that can be used by everyone (Mace, 1998). A voice-activated software program is one example of a specialized accommodation that is used by the general population.

HIGH-TECH ADAPTATIONS

High-tech adaptations are electronically operated or computerized and may include mobility devices such as power wheelchairs, lifts (e.g., an electronic device to transfer an individual from the wheelchair to a bed, bathtub, or other seat), augmentative and alternative communication devices that provide digital or recorded voices for individuals who cannot speak, and environmental control systems that enable an individual to have more control over his or her environment (e.g., remote access to lights, a television, a door, or a fan) (Galvin & Scherer, 1996). These items may be operated through the use of a switch or may be voice activated. Special attention should also be given to the interface requirements when more than one device is being used. For example, if a student uses a power wheelchair and an alternative communication device, consideration of where and how the device will be mounted for the best access is essential. Many of these adaptations provide students access to the school environment itself and are typically requested through the IEP process and funded through educational, medical, or individual insurance funding systems.

LOW-TECH ADAPTATIONS

Low-tech adaptations—those more mechanical in nature—may be commercial or customized. Often, using a commercial item in a different way can solve everyday problems. For example, a battery-operated touch light designed for lighting an area without installing electrical wiring also can be used as a simple communication device to attract someone's attention. Students can brainstorm with their peers who have disabilities about modifications to help students interact with one another more easily—for example, by using simple materials such as Velcro, cardboard, wood, and duct tape to modify existing items to provide a better grip, a more efficient angle, or a clearer view. Students sometimes need an item customized, such as a reinforced bicycle bag equipped with hardware that can be attached to a walker. Other examples include laptrays designed or adapted to place books and papers at adjustable angles, writing utensils with built-up grips for students who have dexterity problems, simple switches that operate slide projectors or other media equipment, and portable stands used to mount magnifiers at a variety of angles.

Special educators who support students in inclusive settings are becoming more proficient at modifying core curriculum, infusing basic skills into daily activities, scheduling staff members and students, and providing other resources to best meet the students' needs. Although many educators are using a range of supports and services to educate students with disabilities and their typically developing peers, many are not sufficiently familiar with assistive technology. The full spectrum of supports and services, including the use of instructional and assistive technologies, should be considered when implementing effective inclusive education practices for students with disabilities. The following story from a middle school classroom illustrates how these technologies have been used to address both belonging and achievement.

Technology in the Classroom

Mr. Diaz's eighth-grade social studies class has been studying a thematic unit titled The Search for Social Justice. Mr. Diaz, one of the more technology-oriented teachers on campus, understands the importance of gaining access to a digital curriculum. He has integrated the use of technology into his strategies, as well as his curriculum, and believes in teaching discrimination between valuable information and drivel found on the Internet. In addition to English, a number of students in his class speak in their native tongue, and at least two students have disabilities. When Mr. Diaz found out that these two students use assistive technology, he was interested in learning about their equipment and how he could accommodate their needs.

Arturo, who recently transferred to the school, has a learning disability that makes it difficult for him to process information auditorily. Arturo, who is shy and soft-spoken, is slow to make friends. Enrolling in school midway through the first semester has made this more difficult for Arturo, who is hesitant to ask for assistance from peers or teachers. Arturo was afraid that he was doomed to isolation in this new environment until Mr. Diaz introduced the students to an eighth-grade class in another state via the Internet. Arturo became interested in participating in this activity because each of Mr. Diaz's students was paired with a student from the other class. The students communicated with their partners via individual e-mail messages and on a class discussion board focused on social justice issues. The parameters had changed; that is, Arturo did not have to respond verbally or immediately, as he was required to do in class. Instead, he could read the messages from his new electronic pal (e-pal) and use the special highlighting features of his screen-reading software, making it easier to follow along visually. He also used word prediction to help increase his typing speed and edited his responses with spell check and grammar check to ensure that his messages were grammatically correct.

Arturo became motivated to participate in this lesson because he found a way to be successful using his own learning style. As his confidence increased, he shared some of his experiences in class and started to make new friends with students whom he had been too shy to approach previously. All of the students' writing skills improved, partly because of the volume of writing that they were exchanging with their e-pals. Not only were the students comparing personal experiences, but they also researched each other's geographical areas on the Internet, improving their abilities to locate and analyze useful information.

The assistive technology served as an equalizer in this scenario. When Arturo was writing to his e-pal, he could use all of the features available to support his reading and writing. On the receiving end, his e-pal saw the finished product, not realizing how long it took Arturo to compose his messages. As Arturo felt more comfortable and competent in using both instructional and assistive technologies, he realized that he might be interested in a career that involved the use of the Internet.

The other student in Mr. Diaz's class who used assistive technology was Kineesha. Unlike Arturo, Kineesha was anything but shy. However, it took teachers many years to see her true personality. When Kineesha was 6 years old, she was placed in a special day class and spent her days with nine other students, none of whom could walk independently, few who could speak more than a few words at a time, and several who had serious health conditions that required the use of oxygen, gastrostomy tubes, and a suctioning apparatus. Needless to say, it was not a stimulating environment, especially for Kineesha, whose smile lit up the room. Although Kineesha could not walk independently or speak full sentences, she clearly had a great deal to say and was eager to learn more about her world. Fortunately, when Kineesha finished first grade, the administrators and teachers at her school became involved in a pilot reform effort that set the school in the direction of providing inclusive education for all students. The day class was disbanded, and all of the students were sent to their neighborhood schools. By the beginning of the fall semester, Kineesha had joined her second-grade peers in Miss Tyler's class, heading in a new direction aided by a full range of supports and modifications, including the introduction of assistive technology.

Her first encounter with the world of assistive technology was through basic switches that helped Kineesha make a connection between cause and effect. An interface box was designed to connect a set of switches to operate a remote-controlled race car. Now, Kineesha could race her car against that of one of the other second-grade students, who was controlling another car with a standard remote. Kineesha used two different colored plate switches, held in place by small suction cups on her laptray. The green switch propelled the car forward, and the red switch shot the car into reverse. After Kineesha understood the connection between her movements and the movement of the car, she learned to use the switches for other toys, appliances, and eventually the computer. Her self-confidence grew and she became eager to try new activities. Her friends realized that with the right connections, both personal and technological, Kineesha was capable of more than they expected.

As Kineesha continued her education, a list of effective switches, seating and positioning recommendations, and other useful assistive technology devices accompanied her to the next grade level. Her teachers were asked to take pictures or videos of Kineesha whenever she mastered a new assistive technology device so that this documentation could be added to her personal portfolio. In addition, examples of the way in which the curriculum was modified and presented to Kineesha were included in her portfolio, as well as samples of her completed assignments and projects. It is common for teachers and families not to record successful strategies, especially when everything is going smoothly. Kineesha's teachers were asked to add lists of things that work and things they wish would have worked but didn't so that undue repetition and frustration might be avoided, or at least limited.

Entering middle school presented new challenges, along with a new environment for Kineesha and her friends. Changing classes, meeting new teachers and students, and attempting to move equipment from class to *class made Kineesha's schedule more complicated. The assistance that she received from her peers in elementary school was more difficult to arrange in middle school because of the number of locations and personnel changes throughout the day, yet Kineesha remained cheerful and positive, and her determination was contagious. Soon, she made new friends, some of whom helped to arrange accommodations for her. Whereas some of these accommodations accompanied Kineesha throughout the day, others were specifically designed for use in different classrooms.*

One of her favorite devices was designed when she was in third grade and was having trouble getting the teacher's attention. Kineesha was not able to raise her hand high like the other children, so a teacher call light was attached to her wheelchair. She operated the light with a small switch that was mounted on a swing-away arm and powered from her wheelchair battery. The light was used to notify others that she wanted to say something through her communication device or that she needed help. Originally, the light was at the end of a brightly colored gooseneck extension so that it could easily be seen from a distance. When Kineesha's teacher commented that the light was too bright, the other students designed paper covers that matched the season, the next holiday, or the thematic unit that they were studying. The whole setup was modified to be less obtrusive as she got older, continuing to fit her age and personality. She intends to give it up by the time she enters ninth grade for something sophisticated that can be operated through her communication device.

Kineesha carries her communication device at all times, as well as a back-up no-tech device that consists of a laminated sheet of cardboard with her most commonly used phrases in the form of Picture Communication Symbols (PCS; available through Mayer-Johnson, Solana Beach, CA, 800-588-4548), photographs, and simple words. The communication device is typically placed on her wheelchair laptray but also can be attached with a mounting system if she is not using her tray or if she moves to a standing position. Some items remain in specific classrooms that help support a range of needs. In English, a tape recorder and pair of headphones are available so that Kineesha can participate in silent reading requirements. In math, she uses a chopstick attached to a special wrist cuff to press the keys of a large talking calculator mounted on a slant board.

During the social justice unit, Kineesha was paired with another student in Mr. Diaz's class to correspond with their assigned e-pal. To complete the research project, Kineesha joined a study group and used the same computer in the library as Arturo—that is, the one that was equipped with the screen-reading software. Although her reading ability is limited, she can help surf the Internet for resources and materials with her peers. While she is improving her switch use and keyboarding skills, the members of her study group take notes or ask her to print out specific pages.

Kineesha also was able to use her switch to operate the multimedia presentation that her group compiled for their culminating experience.

As Kineesha's and Arturo's stories illustrate, consideration of instructional and assistive technologies can help make classrooms more inclusive. The use of CD-ROMs, books on tape, voice-activated software, and access to the Internet through screen readers provides opportunities for students to acquire knowledge and demonstrate their competencies. Technology also can serve as a bridge for communication and for building relationships when students collaboratively work on projects. Researchers are investigating interpersonal connections via computers (Eastmond, 1992; Florini, 1989), raising the notion that more efforts should focus on how to use computers to improve and expand on human contact, rather than negate it (Phillips, 1995). When considering the use of technology to support students with disabilities, the following issues should be given attention.

TECHNOLOGY IS A TOOL, NOT AN END GOAL

For years, students have had IEP goals that target technology skills, such as increasing and improving switch skills. Unfortunately, the student is often scheduled for 15 minutes of switch use in an isolated environment. By approaching switch use as an integrated skill, activities can include participation in the switch-operated multimedia presentation like Kineesha and her group used in social studies. The same logic must apply to instructional technology. For example, students should have access to computers for completing work for all of their classes, not just during computer lab. After all, students are allowed to use their pencils in all classes; why not view the computer as another tool for putting words onto paper? Technology resources often are underused and will remain so until teachers and other school professionals learn the basics. The 1999 National Survey of Teachers' Use of Digital Content, conducted by Education Market Research (see summary of results at www.edweek.org/sreports/tc99/articles/survey.htm), indicated that "53% of all teachers surveyed use software for classroom instruction, and 61% say they use the Internet for instruction" (p. 7). Of those who do not use software for instruction, "75% cite a lack of classroom computers as a reason, and 35% report that they have not had enough training" (p. 39). Clearly, the tools, as well as the expertise, need to be available.

UTILIZE A PERSON-CENTERED ASSESSMENT STRATEGY

Studies show that one of the main reasons individuals do not use assistive technology devices, even when they might be helpful, is that they were not involved in the selection of the equipment (Scherer, 1996). A person-centered assessment approach, as related to the selection of assistive technology, requires that the individual who is going to use the technology not only be involved in the process but actually drive the process. Students need to learn self-advocacy skills at a young age if they are going to gain access to all of the supports, services, and strategies available to help them achieve their goals. Careful consideration must be given to the psychosocial aspects of using the technology. In other words, there must be a match among the student's needs, personality, support system (e.g., family, friends, professionals), and characteristics of the technology itself (Scherer, 1996). Failing to recognize the advantages and disadvantages that a student has for using technology can result in a frustrating process for everyone, with little hope that a good match will be found.

Take, for example, the aesthetics of an assistive technology device. Some students enjoy the attention that accompanies using a device with lights and sounds, whereas others have a difficult time being the center of attention. Family members and peers often are helpful in identifying such details. By involving families in the process, the likelihood of using technology at home also is greater. By involving peers in the process, on-the-spot problem solving occurs on a regular basis. Such critical thinking skills can be incorporated into science and social studies lessons as students are introduced to the use of assistive technology. Invention activities may include the option of designing assistive technology devices or creating new accommodations for peers with disabilities. In any scenario, a holistic approach serves the person and purpose more effectively.

USE TECHNOLOGY AS A BRIDGE
TO ACCOMPLISH A SPECIFIC ACTIVITY

Building on the first two issues, using technology as a bridge to accomplish a specific activity is the next step in the process. Assistive technology devices should not be chosen on the basis of a student's disability but rather should be selected on the basis of the needs, functions, and limitations of that student. It is difficult to buy or design a device if the end goal is not clear. Often, professionals look for devices that are available and then try to mold them to a particular student. This is problematic because if the student's priorities are not considered, as mentioned previously, the device is less likely to be used. A more productive approach is to identify the activity in which the student needs or wishes to participate so that the initial research into existing adaptations can be more fruitful. For example, if a student who does not have any verbal skills must participate in a mock trial as part of a history class, the use of technology could bridge the gap among the student's limitations (no verbal ability), his or her skills (operating a communication device), and the activity of serving as a witness (prerecording a deposition that could be played at appropriate times). Information about such devices is accessible via the Internet by accessing databases (e.g., HyperAbledata) and other assistive technology web sites that include descriptions of communication devices (see the appendix at the end of this chapter).

TAKE ADVANTAGE OF ERGONOMICS, UNIVERSAL DESIGN, AND TALENTED TECHIES

The number of commercially available assistive technology devices exponentially grew during the 1990s. Many items that used to be customized for students with disabilities now are available through generic resources. For example, ergonomically designed computer accessories now are available at office supply stores, furniture stores, and businesses that promote healthy bodies and lifestyles. When more people use such items, they become more affordable. People with and without disabilities can benefit from the use of wrist rests, slant boards, special lighting, foot supports, and adjustable chairs and desks. When specialized modifications still are needed, teachers rarely consider identifying people who have specific skills in carpentry, electronics, mechanical engineering, computers, and general fix-it skills to help with the design and construction of adaptations. A number of programs across the country use volunteers to help develop customized adaptations for individuals with disabilities. Tapping into the resources offered by service organizations (e.g., Kiwanis, Lions, Optimists) can bring additional technical expertise or funding for students who may not qualify for Medicare or insurance funding. Coordinating efforts with technical classes in high schools, community colleges, and universities that require specific projects (e.g., senior projects required in mechanical engineering courses) can provide mutual benefits. Brainstorming takes on a new dimension when engineers share ideas with eighth-grade students and jointly design a project. Although many people assume that assistive technology is expensive, low-tech adaptations can be effective and affordable (Sax et al., 1996).

BE AWARE OF SCHOOL DISTRICT
POLICIES, RESPONSIBILITIES, AND PROCEDURES

When planning for the purchase of any educational technology, school districts must address access issues to meet the current and future needs of students with disabilities. Special education professionals can help by participating on planning teams at the school site and at the district level. The following questions are excerpted from the Tech Pack developed by the U.S. Department of Education, Office of Special Education and Rehabilitative Services. The full document provides a guide for school districts that are trying to provide access to educational technology. It is available on the Internet at www.ed.gov/offices/ OSERS/ tech-pack.html and should prove useful in answering the following questions:

1. How do access barriers to educational technology for students with disabilities differ from access barriers for typically developing students?
2. How can product access for students with disabilities be delivered?
3. Do these input and output alternatives only help students with disabilities?
4. What are a school's legal responsibilities to provide accessible technology for students with disabilities?
5. What is a state's responsibility as a recipient of funds made available under the Technology-Related Assistance for Individuals with Disabilities Act of 1988 (PL 100-407)?
6. How can a school fund educational technology access for students with disabilities?
7. How does a school know whether educational technology products are fully accessible?

Kineesha and Arturo and their teachers, families, and friends discovered that the use of instructional and assistive technologies opened the doors to a more inclusive and successful future. As their teachers observed and explored Kineesha's and Arturo's use of customized and commercial products, they realized the need for ongoing evaluation to ensure that needs continue to be met. The needs, likes, and skills of these students will change as they continue through middle school. As they attend high school and beyond, Kineesha and Arturo likely will outgrow equipment or prefer different features on their devices. The demands and opportunities of new environments will require ongoing examinations of their support strategies to maintain their active involvement in academic coursework and social interactions. More important, they also will build more confidence and take on new responsibilities as they increase their skills. As Kineesha's and Arturo's experiences with assistive technology continue, the opportunities to be valued members of the school and community are limitless.

The world of assistive technology is changing rapidly. As overwhelming as it may seem, it is important to remain current with technological advancements by using the information and resources available through the Internet. Catalogs for special equipment are all but obsolete, as on-line catalogs easily can be accessed and updated on a regular basis. Many companies offer video clips on their web sites or will send out promotional videos free of charge. Although web sites offer many details and resources, users of the Internet must be discriminating in interpreting and applying the information to individual situations.

Appendix

WEB SITES THAT OFFER ASSISTIVE TECHNOLOGY RESOURCES, EQUIPMENT, AND SERVICES

Ablenet — www.ablenetinc.com

Adaptive Environments Center, Inc. — www.adaptenv.org

Alliance for Technology Access — www.ataccess.org

Apple Disability Resources — www.apple.com/disability/welcome.html

Assistive Technology On-line — www.asel.udel.edu

The Center for Universal Design — www.design.ncsu.edu/cud

Closing the Gap — www.closingthegap.com

Computer Access Expertise — home.epix.net/~ansons (click on Denis's page)

Disabilities, Opportunities, Internetworking, and Technology (DO-IT) — www.washington.edu/doit

Equal Access to Software and Information (EASI) — www.isc.rit.edu/~easi

Information and Access Technology Services — www.iatservices.missouri.edu

Matching Person & Technology — members.aol.com/IMPT97/MPT.html

National Center to Improve Practice (Instructional & Assistive Technology) — www.edc.org/FSC/NCIP

Rehabilitation Engineering and Assistive Technology Society of North America (RESNA) — www.resna.org

Tech Connections — www.techconnections.org

Trace Research and Development Center — trace.wisc.edu

United Cerebral Palsy (UCP) — www.ucpa.org/html/resources/index.html

---

The listings included here are current as of November 2000. For more information on local resources, contact your state's Assistive Technology Project.

Untangling the Web—Disability Links	www.icdi.wvu.edu/others.htm#g10
Virtual Assistive Technology Center	www.at-center.com
Web Accessibility Initiative	www.w3.org/WAI/GL

ADDITIONAL RESOURCES

Missouri Technology Center for Special Education
School of Education, Room 24
University of Missouri–Kansas City
5100 Rockhill Road
Kansas City, MO 64110-2499
Voice: (800) 872-7066
Fax: (816) 235-5270
TechCtr@smtpgate.umkc.edu

A quick list for schools to consider when planning what technology to purchase. This is excerpted from a technical assistance packet developed by the Missouri Assistive Technology Project and the Missouri Technology Center for Special Education. (References also can be obtained on the RESNA web site; see web site on page 101.)

Equal Access to Software and Information (EASI)
Project of the Teaching, Learning, and Technology (TLT) Group
(An Affiliate of the American Association for Higher Education)
One Dupont Circle
Suite 360
Washington, DC 20036-1110
Voice: (202) 293-6440
Fax: (202) 293-0073
E-mail: info@aahe.org
www.rit.edu:80/~easi

Students and professionals with disabilities have the same right to gain access to information and resources as everyone else. EASI's mission is to serve as a resource to the education community by providing information and guidance in the area of access-to-information technologies by individuals with disabilities. They stay informed about developments and advancements within the adaptive computer technology field and spread that information to colleges, universities, elementary, middle, and high schools, libraries, and the workplace.

The Computer Accessibility Technology Packet
U.S. Department of Education, Office of Special Education and Rehabilitative Services
600 Independence Avenue, SW
Washington, DC 20202-2500
www.ed.gov/offices/OSERS/techpack.html

The Computer Accessibility Technology Packet was sent by Secretary of Education Richard Riley to state and local education agencies to inform them of their obligations to consider the technology needs of students with disabilities when purchasing hardware, software, and other technological devices.

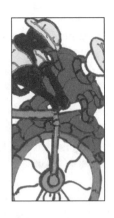

"Never say, I tried it once and it did not work."   *—Lord Ernest Rutherford*

8

Positive Behavior Support

Craig H. Kennedy

Douglas Fisher

ALEXANDRIA

Alexandria (known as Alex) sits quietly at her desk drawing cartoon characters from the television show South Park. Alex's prealgebra teacher, Ms. Foster, calls on her to answer a question, but Alex continues drawing. Her teacher walks to Alex's desk and says, "I asked you a question; please answer me." Alex says something inaudible and continues drawing. Ms. Foster, raising her voice, asks her again to answer the question. Suddenly, Alex jumps from her seat, throws her desk into the student in front of her, and begins screaming and swearing at Ms. Foster.

WHAT IS POSITIVE BEHAVIOR SUPPORT?

School conduct emerged as a highly visible issue in public schools during the 1990s, not only for educators and students but also for families and community members (Walker, Zeller, Close, Webber, & Gresham, 1999).

Reactions to behavior problems at school range from zero tolerance to counseling sessions to benign neglect of the problem. Unfortunately, these approaches have not been successful. In fact, the three most common approaches to school discipline—suspension, counseling, and detention—have repeatedly shown little effect on the occurrence of problem behaviors (Sprague et al., 1998).

A new approach to understanding school discipline problems emerged in the late 1980s (Horner & Carr, 1997). The approach is referred to as positive behavior support and focuses on understanding why students exhibit inappropriate or problem behavior or, more accurate, the social, educational, psychological, and biological reasons behind this behavior. Providing positive behavior support focuses on the bigger picture of a student's life but looks for supporting evidence and specific details that pinpoint reasons that a student acts the way he or she does.

Four elements distinguish positive behavior support from earlier approaches, referred to as *classroom management* or *behavior modification*. First, positive behavior support is nonlinear in its approach to identifying and understanding events that might influence student behavior (Goldiamond, 1974, 1992). A host of events that might affect how a student reacts to occurrences at school or at home are a part of positive behavior support assessments (also called functional assessments). These events include health conditions, likes and dislikes, school history, family life, peer relationships, academic performance, and so forth. This approach looks at a student's behavior as the focal point of a complex web of events that are interrelated in ways that co-influence each other.

Second, positive behavior support is person centered (Scotti & Meyer, 1999), meaning that it focuses on the student from a variety of perspectives. In particular, it brings together information from a range of individuals who know the student in different contexts and asks them to provide, about the student, insights of which others may be unaware. In addition, person-centered approaches look at a student's interests, likes, and dislikes and challenges, within those perspectives, how to facilitate successful progress for the student (Vandercook, York, & Forest, 1989).

Positive behavior support also is analytical. A hallmark of this approach is that specific hypotheses are developed regarding events that influence student behavior (Langland, Lewis-Palmer, & Sugai, 1998; Repp, Felce, & Barton, 1988). In many respects, an assessment of a student's performance using positive behavior support is like a detective story. Evidence is collected and sifted through, then hypotheses are developed and tested to understand why the student is misbehaving. This approach results in a series of testable ideas on why a student is successful or unsuccessful in a certain environment or situation and what can be done to improve his or her performance.

Finally, positive behavior support grounds itself in demonstrating changes in a student's performance. Based on the previous elements identified as characteristic of positive behavior support, interventions that are holistic, contextually sensitive, and hypothesis driven are tested and monitored. If student performance improves, interventions—and the assumptions on which they are based—are viewed as successful. If student performance improves partially or not at all, interventions and their underlying assumptions are reexamined and revised accordingly. This perspective, that problem behaviors are complex and may occur for multiple reasons, allows educators and others to take an interactive approach to solving problems that focus on long-term results.

IMPORTANCE OF AN INTERDISCIPLINARY TEAM APPROACH

Given the goals and elements of positive behavior support, an overarching theme emerges—this approach only makes sense within a framework of interdisciplinary collaboration. Because this approach focuses on bringing together multiple perspectives regarding a student's appropriate and inappropriate behavior, the various individuals with whom a student interacts are necessary contributors and participants in this process. This makes cooperation and collaboration among a variety of professionals, paraprofessionals, administrators, family, and community members an integral part of a successful positive behavior support plan.

Problem behaviors occur for many reasons and require multiple types of expertise to identify. Family members and the student can offer perspectives on the student's history, important life events, and current challenges and strengths of which professionals are sometimes unaware. Educators offer a perspective that focuses on the student's current academic and social functioning within specific curriculum and instructional contexts. Health professionals are able to identify health care needs and explain how to effectively address them. Administrators provide policy insights and leadership. Psychologists provide information on the underlying causes of appropriate and inappropriate behavior. In addition, there are other people, including case managers, related services professionals, and community leaders, who, depending on a student's needs, can provide insights into the student's life.

Because of the important but diverse perspectives for understanding problem behavior, an emerging model of positive behavior support focuses on schoolwide support teams (Kennedy et al., 2000). This approach asks schools, rather than individual teachers, to take responsibility for students who present challenging behavior. Historically, classroom teachers have been responsible for student conduct in the classroom. Apart from curricular decisions made at the departmental or school level, the way that a teacher arranges classroom management, systematic instruction, and grading was his or her own responsibility. However, with the growing realization that more and more diverse students are attending school with the expectation of succeeding, the teacher as captain of his or her own ship is becoming something of the past. Replacing this historical notion is the teacher as the focal point of a schoolwide team of professionals working together to deliver instruction (Mac Iver, 1990). A classroom teacher may be the one who delivers curriculum and instruction but within the context of multiple individuals' planning and making decisions about those classroom activities.

Schoolwide teams meet needs that have not explicitly been addressed by earlier approaches to dealing with behavior problems. One area of need is to place responsibility for students with behavior problems at the administrative level rather than at the classroom level. By doing this, schools and communities, rather than individual teachers, take responsibility for a student's success. A second need is for multiple types of expertise to be involved in the planning and teaching process. As previously noted, behavior problems occur for many reasons that span a variety of disciplines and perspectives (e.g., medicine, psychology, curriculum, instruction, case management). Finally, multiple areas of expertise and schoolwide responsibility require school teams to coordinate activities. Teaming allows for greater integration of perspectives, a mechanism for monitoring support strategies, and a forum to share decisions. Given the importance of this approach, the remainder of this chapter discusses the use of positive behavior support within the context of school teams.

CONDUCTING FUNCTIONAL ASSESSMENTS

Texts on conducting functional assessments recommend beginning with a review of the student's records (Carr et al., 1994; O'Neill et al., 1994; Scotti & Meyer, 1999). Examples of information to look for include previous educational placements, current and past IEPs, reason(s) that referrals were given for behavior problems, previous interventions, history of special health care needs, and types of disabilities (Kennedy & Thompson, 2000). Once this information is gathered, an interdisciplinary team meeting is called to discuss the student and his or her behavior.

Kennedy and Thompson (2000) suggested that the first meeting focus on several key issues relating to establishing an overall context for why the student may exhibit behavior problems. During the first team meeting, the people who know the student should focus on defining the student's strengths, his or her preferences and interests, his or her support needs and areas of concern, and the types of curricular and instructional experiences that the student is receiving. The goal of this initial meeting is to assess the student not in terms of his or her behavior problems but within the context of larger issues in his or her life (see Vandercook et al., 1989, for a related approach). The information gathered allows team members to better understand the student's strengths and needs and the structure of his or her school day.

Once members have initially met and the student's school day has been reviewed, an assessment of the student's curriculum and instruction should occur. Research suggests that the cause of approximately 80% of behavior problems is in curriculum and instruction (Dunlap & Kern, 1993; Scotti & Meyer, 1999). Hence, the initial focus of assessment is on this constellation of events. In particular, teachers, related services personnel, and administrators should focus on identifying the degree to which current, recommended practices are used as the basis of instruction. This process is inherently evaluative and provides the opportunity for teachers to reflect on their own teaching practices and look for areas to improve.

Table 8.1 lists 14 commonly accepted practices that are indicative of quality classroom practices (see also Chapter 3) and includes brief descriptions of what these practices entail. Some teachers reflect on their own teaching practices or have another individual assess their teaching to establish the degree to which each of the practices is being implemented on a consistent basis. Areas that have been demonstrated to be of particular relevance to the occurrence of problem behavior include 1) following a functional and meaningful curriculum, 2) making choices, 3) specifying preferences, 4) attending to appropriate student behavior, and 5) using predictable schedules for classroom and school activities. The extent to which these are used is directly related to the occurrence of problem behavior (Dunlap & Kern, 1993). However, these proactive teaching strategies are part of a larger set of variables that require assessment when developing a positive behavior support plan.

After times and places in which curricular changes can be made are assessed, additional information is gathered about other events that might be related to problem behavior (O'Neill et al., 1994). Typically, team members follow a structured interview that is used to gather information about 1) types of problem behaviors, 2) the presence of special health care needs, 3) the stability of the living situation, and 4) people, places, times, and activities associated with the occurrence and nonoccurrence of behavior problems. This information allows team members

Table 8.1. Fourteen best practices for classroom instruction

Recommended, best practice	Brief description
Meaningful and functional curriculum	Is the material being taught to the student useful to him or her and relevant to his or her daily life? Providing a meaningful and functional curriculum is an important means of increasing student motivation to work with instructional materials.
Facilitating membership	Do students with and without disabilities have regular, daily opportunities to interact and develop relationships with each other? Frequent social interactions with other students allow for relationship development and improve students' social competence.
Providing choices	Are students allowed to actively choose the focus and content of instructional materials? This component is important because it increases students' interest in instructional materials and allows them to actively choose some of the content of their curriculum.
Varying instructional materials	Are the means by which instructional materials presented to students varied from period to period and day to day? Actively varying the means by which students contact instructional materials improves their attention during instruction and their learning.
Implementing age appropriate materials	Are the materials and content that are being taught to students something that their typically developing peers frequently use? This is important because it provides students with relevant instructional experiences that they can relate to their peers.
Attending to positive student behavior	Are students provided with attention from teachers primarily for engaging in appropriate and desirable behavior? The provision of teacher attention for appropriate behavior is important because it teaches students in which behaviors they should engage.
Predicting schedules	Is each student able to understand and predict in which activities he or she is being asked to engage? Making educational routines predictable allows students to understand why they are being asked to terminate an activity, what will be occurring next, and what they will receive for participating.

Learning strategies for groups	Are a variety of group learning strategies used as a means for students to learn instructional material? Providing students with regular opportunities to learn to cooperate and interact with each other is an effective means of increasing learning.
Incorporating learning styles	Different students have different patterns of learning and engaging in instructional materials. Do teaching strategies accommodate for individual students? This is important to do, because it allows each student to receive maximum benefit from instruction.
Focusing on student	Do student interests and preferences provide the basis for instructional content? This is important because students are less likely to emit problem behavior when they are engaged in activities that they like to do.
Modeling appropriate behavior	Do teachers and peers actively model how students should behave for them to be more effective learners? Modeling is a very effective means of teaching students and allows them to see others engaging in successful and appropriate learning experiences.
Using student-based interdisciplinary teams	Are teachers and administrators using school-based teams to work collectively on improving the behavior of students? Working as a team provides a variety of perspectives, experiences, and skills to be brought together to solve problems and proactively plan.
Knowing medications	Are any students receiving medication that might affect their behavior? Teachers need to know what the primary effects, side effects, and long-term effects of a medication are so they can monitor its impact on student performance.
Knowing special health care needs	Do students have any identified or suspected special health care needs? Students should be monitored regularly for special health care needs and receive regular checkups from health personnel, especially prior to the development of a positive behavior support plan, to assess for the existence of possible health care issues relating to problem behavior.

to develop ideas about why problem behaviors may be occurring, often referred to in the positive behavior support literature as hypotheses. These hypotheses are developed by looking at the pattern of when problem behaviors do and do not occur and what events precede and follow the behaviors of concern. This allows team members to generate ideas about the conditions associated with the student's appropriate and inappropriate actions.

Once information has been collected by team members relating to 1) student strengths and needs, 2) curriculum and instructional issues, and 3) hypotheses regarding the causes of problem behavior, direct observation is used to assess the occurrences and nonoccurrences of problem behavior (Carr et al., 1994; O'Neill et al., 1994). These observations occur in the settings in which the student typically is found. Information is collected by teachers or related services personnel for 1–2 weeks (allowing multiple observations in each setting). The direct observation information is summarized in terms of when, where, how often, and why problem behaviors occurred. That information is compared with information gathered earlier. The goal of the assessment process is to identify the circumstances under which the student appropriately and inappropriately behaves so a better picture can be gleaned about why the student engages in problem behavior.

DEVELOPING POSITIVE
BEHAVIOR SUPPORT STRATEGIES

The information gathered during the assessment is analogous to clues that a detective collects to solve a mystery. Pieces of information yield important details regarding why problem behaviors occur and, just as important, why appropriate behaviors occur. For example, knowing that a student behaves appropriately in math, English, and science but misbehaves in social studies suggests something may be occurring (or not occurring) in this last class that is the source of the problem behavior. The functional assessment process allows gathering of information to identify why problem behavior occurs.

Perusing the functional assessment data for clues involves starting with several broad areas to identify events that contribute to behavior problems and then synthesizing this information for overall patterns of behavior. At the broadest level, the assessment information should identify 1) curricular and instructional events that are associated and not associated with the occurrence of problem behavior, 2) the presence of biological events that contribute to behavior problems (e.g., menstruation, sleep disorders, changes in psychotropic medication), and 3) typical outcomes associated with the occurrence of behavior problems (e.g., changes in routine or social interactions). Each of these categories can, and often does, play a role in the overall pattern of why problem behaviors do and do not occur.

Once these broader events have been assessed for patterns, the data are scrutinized by team members at a finer-grained level for additional patterns. In particular, team members look for 1) problem behaviors actually occurring, 2) behaviors occurring together, in clusters, or in sequences, 3) antecedent events that are present when behavior problems occur (e.g., particular types of tasks or the presence of certain people), 4) changes as a result of the problem behavior (in terms of classroom practices, teacher behavior, or the student's situation), and 5) the social function of the problem behavior (e.g., escaping difficult tasks, gaining peer attention) (Luiselli & Cameron, 1998; O'Neill et al., 1994; Reichle & Wacker, 1993).

As a collection, this information will identify specific places, times, activities, and social contexts in which a pattern of appropriate and inappropriate behavior emerges. For example, if a student exhibits problem behavior only during social studies, then that pattern suggests something may be different about the social studies class. The difference will be revealed through the types of information gathered. Is social studies a preferred or nonpreferred content subject? What types of recommended curriculum and instruction practices are used in this class? Is there any reason to believe that biological issues (e.g., fatigue, use of medication) may be related to the time that the class is offered? What are the specific events that occur right before and after the problem behavior? How are the student's activities in the class altered as a result of the problem behavior?

The goal of this process is to develop hypotheses about why problem behaviors occur. Such hypotheses should identify when, where, why, and who is related to problem behavior. Identifying this pattern suggests the strategies that should be developed to counter the problem situations (Repp et al., 1988). Following up on the social studies example, if the student's problem behavior was found to be associated with group learning activities, hypotheses might be developed about why those specific situations lead to behavior problems. For instance, it might be found that problem behaviors occur only when a particular peer is part of the learning group and that these two students have a history of negative interactions.

Within the positive behavior support process, this information becomes the foundation for building an intervention (formally known as a positive behavior support plan). Hypotheses regarding the conditions under which problem behaviors occur specify conditions that can be changed. Typically, interventions are classified as focusing on

1) curriculum and instruction, 2) biological concerns, and 3) skill development. Interventions relating to curriculum and instruction focus on making changes to the instructional arrangements that the student experiences. Biological concerns are a focus of health professionals. Skill development–based interventions focus on building a student's ability to successfully deal with challenging situations. Deciding which approach (or some combination thereof) is selected for the positive behavior support plan depends on the hypotheses regarding why problem behavior occurs. To illustrate this hypothesis-driven process, we look at the social studies example. The student's problem behaviors were associated with the social studies class, group learning activities, and the presence of a specific peer within those groups. On the basis of this differential pattern of problem behavior, an intervention may deal with curriculum and instructional arrangements (e.g., having the students work in different groups) or skill development (e.g., teaching the students conflict-resolution skills).

The positive behavior support approach to identifying why problem behaviors occur as a basis for intervention development is not a traditional, formulaic approach to dealing with problem behaviors. In the past, a teacher consulted a book on behavior modification or classroom management and selected an intervention that seemed appropriate (often classified by its level of intrusiveness) without reference to why the problem behavior was occurring. The theory behind positive behavior support, however, places the cause(s) of the behavior first, focuses on identifying those causes, and then allows that information to specify the form of intervention (O'Neill et al., 1994; Reichle & Wacker, 1993; Scotti & Meyer, 1999).

DEVELOPING A POSITIVE
BEHAVIOR SUPPORT FOR ALEXANDRIA

Because Alex engages in problem behaviors, she is at risk for a more restrictive educational placement. Therefore, the first step in conducting a functional assessment of her behavior is to review her student records. Alex's records indicate that her teachers had intermittent concerns about her behavior when she was in elementary school but that the intensity of those problems varied from year to year. Reasons for this variability were not mentioned. She has maintained grade-level performance, her educational and home placements have been stable, and her health has been good. Currently, she is in her first year of middle school (sixth grade). The first month or so of school was fine, but problem behaviors emerged quickly after that. Because she is failing some subjects and her behavior is becoming more aggressive, her team has decided to develop a behavior support plan for Alex.

In the initial meeting, a behavioral psychologist walks the team members through an interview designed to identify when, where, and why problem behaviors are occurring (O'Neill et al., 1994). The team identifies the following problem behaviors as concerns: drawing at her desk, talking to herself, ignoring adults, and verbal and physical aggression. The first three behaviors occur daily, the aggression occurs weekly, and the behaviors occur in a sequence from internalizing behaviors to verbal aggression to physical aggression. With input from the school nurse and teachers, it is determined that Alex does not have any medical conditions and, because she is not taking any medication, drug side effects are not a concern.

Further into the interview, it is noted that she does not engage in problem behaviors in every class; instead, the problems typically appear in physical education (PE) and math. In her other classes, she is doing fine (behaviorally and academically), although her teachers note that she requires prompting and they have to be aware of her good days and bad days. During the interview, teachers are asked to self-evaluate their teaching practices (see Table 9.1). It is noted that, generally, her classes provide 80% or more of the best practices listed in the table. However, the two classes in which her problem behaviors are occurring use fewer than 30% of the best practices (although the type of practices varied among the classes). The team realizes that the PE and math teachers both are new to the school; the PE teacher is a first-year teacher, and the math teacher transferred from a private school.

The team decides to collect direct observation information to identify whether a differential pattern of behavior exists among classrooms and to establish possible antecedents to problem behaviors, as well as generate possible hypotheses regarding why Alex engages in these behaviors. After collecting information for a week, the team meets again. The direct observation data support the pattern first identified in the interview—Alex's problems were occurring primarily in PE and math. It is noted that specific instructional situations were associated with problem behaviors. In PE, problems typically occurred either when students were completing worksheets (which was the focus of instruction twice per week) or during free day (when students individually chose what to do). In math, problems arose during didactic instruction followed by in-seat work assignments. Further discussion of the data by team members identified events consistently followed by problem behaviors. First, Alex typically avoided having to do worksheets or in-seat assignments (she was sent into the hallway for time-out). Second, her verbal and physical confrontations with teachers typically resulted in peer attention (e.g., "You can't say that to the teacher").

Team members agreed that the focus of concern was primarily curriculum and instruction issues. To address these concerns, the team developed the following recommendations. First, a tenured teacher would begin to mentor the first-year PE teacher. He or she would serve as a resource for the younger teacher, observe the younger teacher's classroom, provide feedback to him or her, and be available for advice. Second, the mentoring pair would develop a plan to increase the younger teacher's implementation of best practices in his PE program, including increasing the functionality of the academic curriculum to be more embedded within sport activities (and not be separate, seatwork assignments), to review class rules before each class, and to provide more structure during the daily PE class. Another mentor was established for the math teacher; this pair decided that more group work, particularly within cooperative learning arrangements, would be tried in the class. In addition, the math teacher agreed to provide friendly prompts to Alex on a regular basis during class to help her identify when she was working hard and to keep her on task if she was having a difficult day. Third, Alex's peers in PE and math were asked to ignore her outbursts, with the rationale that she should not act that way and others should not feed into her problem behaviors.

As a collection, these strategies were implemented and maintained throughout Alex's sixth-grade year. The changes in PE resulted in substantial decreases in problem behavior. In math, several additional changes were needed before Alex's performance stabilized. These efforts focused primarily on a twice-a-week after-school tutor to help Alex improve her math performance; once she was back to grade level, her problem behaviors were greatly reduced.

Positive behavior support provides an alternative approach for understanding school conduct problems. Prior to the development of positive behavior support and its incorporation into the IDEA Amendments of 1997, eliminative strategies to behavior problems were the preferred approaches. That is, interventions were developed to reduce or eliminate problem behaviors as the primary focus (labeled behavior modification, consequences, or classroom management). Unfortunately, by their nature, these approaches tended to use punishment to suppress behavioral concerns and did not take into account the sources of the behavior problems. Positive behavior support, as an alternative, focuses on why the behavior problems are occurring and inductively builds on this to provide students with alternatives to inappropriate behavior.

As outlined in this chapter, positive behavior support begins with a school team approach. This team approach brings together teachers, administrators, related services personnel, family, and community members who each have some knowledge and area of expertise relating to the student whose behavior is of concern. With this diversified knowledge, a series of assessments are conducted to identify 1) the student's strengths, interests, and support needs, 2) the degree to which the student's classroom experiences are providing him or her with curriculum and instruction based on best practices, 3) what the specific behaviors of concern are, 4) the presence of any special health care needs that may influence student performance, 5) the times, places, people, and activities associated with appropriate and inappropriate behavior, and 6) what the student's misbehavior avoids or obtains.

This assessment process informs educators about why the student's problem behaviors are occurring. With this information, team members can develop support strategies based on individual student need. Typically, support plans include changing curriculum and instruction, developing a student's social competence, addressing health needs more effectively, and systematically monitoring student progress. These interventions flow inductively from the assessment information and are based on areas of need, as well as on strengths of the student and teachers.

Another important aspect of positive behavior support is that once intervention plans are developed, their implementation is a team process. Not only do team members meet and assess student progress with the positive behavior support plan, but it is implemented (to the degree necessary) by each of the individuals who come into contact with the student. This provides a broad basis for intervention, multiple areas of expertise, and a support system not only for the student but also for the various individuals who work with the student on a regular basis.

Although they may seem of recent origin, positive behavior support plans are the cumulative product of more than 30 years of research and development (for more detailed information, see issues of the *Journal of Positive Behavior Interventions*). The approach is based on assessments of why behaviors of concern are occurring; this distinguishes positive behavior supports from previous behavior change strategies. This approach is being demonstrated to be effective not only for students with disabilities but also for any student who engages in problem behavior. That success is, in part, due to the comprehensive assessment of why problem behaviors occur and the hypotheses that are derived from this information. Also, it is due to the range of variables that can be incorporated into interventions and the team-based approach to behavior change.

"Treat people as if they were what they ought to be, and you help them to become what they are capable of being."
—*Johann Wolfgang von Goethe*

9

Tying It Together
Personal Supports that Lead to Membership and Belonging

Nancy Frey

The final ingredient to ensure access to general education classrooms and core curriculum for all students is personal supports. Through personal supports, the necessary curriculum accommodations and modifications are created and delivered. Through personal supports, assistive technology is used and refined to meet the tasks at hand. Through personal supports, membership and belonging are facilitated for all students. Indeed, personal supports represent, as New York Yankees baseball great Reggie Jackson said, "The straw that stirs the drink."

Personal supports are necessary for all students. These supports can be classified into two groups: *natural supports* and *specialized supports*. Natural supports, such as the classroom teacher and peers, are available to all students enrolled in a class. Schoolwide natural supports include the guidance counselor, school resource officer, school psychologist,

119

reading specialist, and social worker. These generic supports, already in place in most schools, often are overlooked as sources for students with disabilities in favor of more expensive, categorical special education supports. Specialized supports represent a more intensive level of personal supports. These include the services of special education teachers, paraprofessionals, and behavioral support personnel. Paraprofessionals from other categorical programs, such as Title I and English Language Development for English Language Learners (ELD/ELL), also are included. Related services specialists such as speech-language therapists, occupational and physical therapists, orientation and mobility specialists, vision specialists, translators, and audiologists represent additional specialized supports. These specialists should provide their services within general education classrooms. If this is not possible, they should provide services at a time that is least disruptive to instruction.

It is important to view personal supports as on a continuum. As a supplemental service, special education was designed to move students along this continuum to increase their independence. Roles and responsibilities must be redefined in order to maximize the availability and flexibility of these personal supports. Role negotiations are a critical component in school reform agendas and should be viewed as a way of ensuring student success.

UTILIZING SPECIALIZED
AND NATURAL SUPPORT STAFF

Students require varying amounts and types of specialized staff resources to be successful (see Table 9.1 for a summary of the range of personnel support options). Some students require *total staff support*. Special educators and paraprofessionals often provide this level of support. The staff person is often in close proximity to the student and may assist with the necessary materials and supplies to complete class assignments and group work. The staff member models cooperation, collaboration, and respect. This person also facilitates relationships between students with and without disabilities. Specialized support is usually necessary initially for students who, for example, require full-time oxygen, use feeding tubes, or need behavioral support. However, because the continued presence of adults can create social barriers that inhibit independence, educators and parents should actively create opportunities for natural supports (Giangreco, Edelman, Luiselli, & MacFarland, 1997).

As students learn the routines and customs of a class, the support staff members move to a *part-time* or *intermittent support* strategy. This involves special educators and paraprofessionals' providing in-class assistance at predetermined times or checking in on classrooms on a

Table 9.1.   Levels of student support

Total staff support	The staff person remains seated in close proximity to the student. Support staff may need to assist the student with materials and supplies needed to complete class assignments and group work. The staff member provides a role model for cooperation, collaboration, acceptance, and respect for all.
Part-time support	The support staff provide assistance to a student at a predetermined time or on a rotating basis. The staff person maintains an awareness of curriculum and assignments to encourage student productivity, completion of assignments, and tutorial or organizational support.
Intermittent support	The support staff (peer support, natural support, and paid staff) provide assistance in the classrooms on a daily or every-other-day basis to troubleshoot immediate challenges and to assist with surprise assignments or projects.
Peer tutor	Peer tutors provide support to the student in a variety of ways. They may assist in mobility to and from class, carrying or remembering materials, taking notes, assisting with completing assignments, facilitating communication, and being a role model for social and friendship interactions. The peer tutors also may participate in the development of support strategies. The peer tutor receives five elective credits for providing this support.
Natural support	This type of support is provided by students who are enrolled in the class. This student usually volunteers to provide support by taking notes, recording homework assignments, and so forth.
Supplemental support	This support is provided by speech-language therapists, orientation and mobility specialists, and physical and occupational therapists. They provide their services within general education classrooms.

regular basis. The staff person continues his or her awareness of curriculum and assignments and also may provide assistance and direction to peer tutors as needed.

Natural supports, including classmates, peer tutors, and teacher assistants, are available to any student in the class. Classmates often assist with mobility, notetaking, role modeling, and facilitating groups. Peer tutors report to a specific teacher and complete a range of assignments, including providing support to students with disabilities who are enrolled in the class. They often also serve to connect the student with disabilities to other students, although they should not replace a student's need for friends (Kennedy et al., 1997; Whitaker, Barratt, Thomas, Potter, & Joy, 1998). At some schools, students can enroll in a teacher assistant class. This elective class is open to all students, and assistants usually recruit their friends for future semesters. The ability to gain access to natural supports in an environment should be a central goal for students with disabilities. It is important that students with disabilities learn to rely on natural supports while they are in school so that they can be comfortable with these kinds of supports once they are adults and can use them in the workplace.

REDEFINING EDUCATIONAL ROLES

As schools move toward more inclusive practice, the processes of the past often no longer meet the needs of students, teachers, and administrators. Practitioners may find themselves being asked to provide services to a new group of students and staff. In evolving schools, mistaken assumptions can arise regarding the roles and responsibilities of each member of the team, which can result in gaps in school and district procedures and services to students. Who should complete the report card? Which team member schedules parent conferences? Which department is responsible for monitoring district completion requirements so that the student can matriculate to high school? These oversights can lead to misunderstandings and even legal action if not addressed proactively.

Special educators, in particular, are undergoing a metamorphosis within the profession. Many were trained in categorical programs that emphasized educating students with a particular disability, with little focus on the commonalities of teaching all students. Furthermore, special educators were expected to provide services within a specific service delivery model, such as a resource room or a self-contained classroom. Few experiences within the general education curriculum were offered in the teacher preparation programs of the past.

The Role of a Special Educator in an Inclusive School

Today, special educators are being prepared for inclusive classrooms and schools. The practitioners in the field, who are redefining their roles in these innovative schools, are guiding their preparation. Their practice now focuses on instruction, assessment, communication, leadership, and record keeping (see Table 9.2).

Instruction Special educators provide individual and small-group instruction as they always have, but now they do so in inclusive schools, where it is more broadly defined. A special educator may be assigned to a general education classroom to reteach key concepts to a group of students with and without disabilities. They also may coteach the class with the content area teacher, therefore instructing the whole class. Students with disabilities in general education also may require accommodations and modifications of assignments and assessments, and this is the responsibility of the special educator. As the primary implementer of the student's IEP, the special educator also monitors academic work and coordinates support for individuals, including behavioral and medical needs.

Assessment Administration of educational tests and inventories is an important duty for the special educator. The interpretation and application of the results of these instruments also fall to the special education teacher. In the classroom, grading students' performance on assignments and teacher-designed tests may be collaboratively done with the general educator. In addition, the special educator assists students in developing appropriate demonstrations of their work, including culminating projects and student exhibitions.

Communication The special educator in an inclusive school facilitates communication among families, staff, and administrators. Curricular, technological, and personal supports for students with IEPs are dependent on timely and accurate exchanges of information. These communications occur in planning and problem-solving meetings, as well as through conversations and written communication with families. The special educator also provides information about inclusive practices to staff and administrators. Many inclusion support teachers find it helpful to establish tools consistently used for communication, including the creation of an assistance request form to be used by the general education team. The infused skills grid, student profile, and academic unit lesson plan (AULP) all are used to exchange information.

Leadership Today's special educators play an important leadership role on inclusive campuses. Supervision and training of paraprofessionals who provide personal supports remain roles of the special educator, but this now extends throughout the school community. Many schools administer peer-tutoring classes for elective credits to provide assistance to other students. Special educators may teach these peer-tutoring classes and coordinate peer-tutoring assignments. Also, they encourage the development of natural supports and friendships by observing interactions, modeling support strategies, and then fading prompts to allow the natural supports to emerge. Finally, special educators demonstrate leadership when they collaborate with related services providers, such as speech-language pathologists and physical therapists, to identify opportunities in the student's schedule to provide services.

Record Keeping There is a long tradition of extensive paperwork in special education. The special educator develops and main-

Table 9.2.   The role of the special educator in an inclusive school

Instruction	Assessment	Communication	Leadership	Record keeping
Instructing individual students	Grading students' performance	Attending planning meetings	Training and supervising paraprofessionals	Developing the IEP
Adapting materials and instruction	Developing appropriate exhibitions and demonstrations of student work	Communicating with parents and families	Coordinating peer tutors	Maintaining records of student performance
Providing small-group instruction	Administering educational tests	Attending problem-solving meetings	Facilitating the use of related-services professionals	Maintaining records of curriculum accommodations and modifications
Teaching the whole class		Providing information about inclusion		
Monitoring students' academic work				
Coordinating support (including medical and behavioral needs) for individual students				

tains the IEP and ensures that all general educators receive a copy and understand it (the infused skills grid and student profile can assist in this endeavor). Also, they maintain records of the student's performance, including progress toward IEP goals. To ensure accurate grading and class credits, records of accommodations and modifications provided to students must be kept. This can be done through the use of the unit lesson plan.

Technology has allowed the special educator to complete tasks more efficiently. Communication tools and lesson plans are commonly transmitted over school-based e-mail to ensure speedy delivery of information. Templates of forms can be placed on the school's server to make these tools available throughout the school. Electronic communication also allows teachers to make up-to-the-minute changes in schedules and paraprofessional assignments.

The Role of a General Educator in an Inclusive School

Like the special educator, today's teacher faces change in the classroom. Although many teaching duties remain unchanged, the students often are quite different. Students with diverse learning needs, including those with disabilities, are seen by nearly every educator. Support staff, including special educators, therapists, and paraprofessionals, are assigned to these new students. The philosophy of redistributing compensatory program funds from special education and Title I throughout the school means that staff who formerly had little interaction may now be communicating on a daily basis.

Clearly defined roles and responsibilities are necessary for effective educational teams. Like the special educator, the general education teacher has instructional, assessment, communication, leadership, and record-keeping duties (see Table 9.3); however, the ways in which they are carried out differ.

Instruction   Principle instruction of all assigned students remains a central job responsibility of the general educator. In inclusive classrooms, the population of students has broadened to include a wide range of abilities. This diversity challenges content area teachers to utilize their repertoire of instructional arrangements, including individual and small-group instruction, as well as traditional large-group delivery. Students must be monitored for academic progress, as always, but the general educator uses this information in collaboration with other support personnel to identify and implement necessary adaptations to ensure continued growth.

Assessment   Assessments fall into three categories: classroom, standardized, and performance based. The general educator has the responsibility for conducting all of the assessments. Classroom formative

Table 9.3. The role of the general educator in an inclusive school

Instruction	Assessment	Communication	Leadership	Record keeping
Instructing individual students Providing small-group instruction Teaching the whole class Monitoring students' academic progress Implementing accommodations and modifications designed by the special educator	Conducting formative and summative assessments of students, including grading assignments and projects Administering local and state standardized tests Developing appropriate exhibitions and demonstrations of student work	Collaborating with the special educator on the curriculum for the class Providing feedback on the effectiveness of strategies Attending IEP and planning meetings Communicating with families and parents	Designing the structure of the class, including curriculum, classroom management policies, physical design, and the selection of materials Supervising para-professionals and peer tutors assigned to the class Providing information to grade-level teams on curriculum and instruction	Recording the unit and daily lesson plans, activities, and homework Maintaining student grade and attendance records Attending problem-solving meetings

and summative assessments are used to monitor progress and determine mastery of content. In some instances, these assessments and grades may be determined collaboratively with the special educator.

State and district standardized tests are increasing in importance in many states, and the inclusion of special education students in these assessments is an important feature of the IDEA Amendments of 1997, commonly called IDEA '97. Most students with disabilities can take these tests with or without allowable accommodations. The IEP committee determines the need for these accommodations, as well as those needed for classroom assessments.

Student exhibitions and demonstrations compose performance-based assessment. The general educator helps students develop these projects and portfolios and implements adaptations designed by the special educator.

Communication   Sound decision making is dependent on timely and accurate information. The ability to share this information is essential in inclusive schools. As with all communication, the responsibility falls to each team member. The general educator is responsible for providing the special education teacher with curriculum, materials, and unit plans in a timely fashion so that necessary accommodations and modifications can be developed. Without this exchange of information, students with IEPs cannot fully participate in the classroom. This creates frustration for staff, parents, and the student and often can be prevented when time is allocated and procedures are followed consistently.

The general educator also provides feedback to the special educator on the effectiveness of strategies. What may look like a great accommodation on paper could be inadequate when used in the classroom. Identifying what works and what does not work refines teaching practices. Families and parents should also be a part of the communication loop, and all professionals who deal with a student should be careful to communicate their goals and progress to the child's family.

Leadership   The structure and design of the classroom, including curriculum, materials, and physical layout, are the responsibility of the general educator. Classroom management policies also are designed and taught by the content area teacher. In all of these aspects, the special educator can be a valuable resource of ideas and strategies that will effectively support students with IEPs in the classroom.

The general education teacher supervises paraprofessionals and peer tutors assigned to the classroom. These specialized supports are made available for students with IEPs who require additional assistance, and it is essential that these supports complement the instructional routines of the class. The general educator gives immediate feedback and direction to paraprofessionals and tutors so that these resources are used wisely.

The leadership duties of the general education teacher extend to the grade level or content area team as well. Many schools require that all staff participate in regularly scheduled planning meetings to discuss curriculum and instruction. In inclusive schools, these teams include special educators so that information can more easily be exchanged.

Record Keeping   The general educator is responsible for recording unit and daily lesson plans, activities, and homework. In addition, he or she maintains the students' grades and attendance records.

The Role of a Paraprofessional in an Inclusive School

Once rare in school, paraprofessionals are becoming a common sight in contemporary classrooms. Sometimes, parents and educators mistakenly assume that the presence of another adult is all that is needed to sufficiently support a student. Like the other team members, a paraprofessional in an inclusive school needs clearly defined roles and responsibilities in order for these supports to happen. These duties include instruction, assessment, communication, leadership, and record keeping (see Table 9.4).

Instruction   The primary instructional responsibilities of the paraprofessional are to implement lesson plans as designed by the general education teacher and to deliver accommodations and modifications as designed by the special educator. Paraprofessionals are not responsible for delivering primary instruction to a student. However, the paraprofessional can reteach skills to individuals and small groups that need additional time and experience with the material. A paraprofessional in an inclusive classroom provides specialized support on an as-needed basis to students with IEPs and general support to the rest of the class as directed by the content area teacher. A common error among paraprofessionals is providing support only to a specific student or students. When specialized supports are necessary for a particular student, the classroom teacher should clearly communicate the nature, duration, and frequency of these supports.

Assessment   Although assessment is the responsibility of the teacher, the paraprofessional plays an important role in measuring student progress by assisting and supporting the teacher, especially with classroom logistics and student preparation. Paraprofessionals also are important sources of information on mastery. They collaborate with the general and special educators to report student progress, as observed in their interactions with students.

Communication   Paraprofessionals provide feedback to the teachers on the success of the strategies used and make suggestions about

Table 9.4. The role of the paraprofessional in an inclusive school

Instruction	Assessment	Communication	Leadership	Record keeping
Following instructional plans as implemented by the general education teacher	Assisting and supporting the teacher with the assessment of student performance	Providing feedback to team members on the success of strategies	Facilitating social relationships between students	Maintaining logs and time sheets as required to document contact time
Implementing accommodations and modifications as designed by the special educator	Collaborating with the general and special education teachers to report student progress	Assisting the teachers in communication with parents and families	Creating a positive and reinforcing environment for students	
Providing specialized assistance to assigned students as necessary, including personal care		Maintaining effective and open communication with school personnel	Modeling effective communication strategies for other staff	
Reteaching skills to individuals and small groups		Honoring confidentiality of student information		

possible improvements. They also assist the teachers in communicating with parents and families. Because the paraprofessional often works closely with a particular student, questions about the student's progress may be directed to him or her. In order to ensure that the information given is consistent and accurate, these inquiries should be referred to the teachers.

Because they work in a variety of classrooms throughout the day, paraprofessionals also are responsible for maintaining effective and open communication with other school personnel. Although important information may be shared to facilitate effective supports, it is essential that the confidentiality of the students be honored.

Leadership   Paraprofessionals often work closely with students with disabilities and can have a great impact on their school lives. Their presence can influence the social climate for the student among peers and other staff. The paraprofessional facilitates social relationships between students to allow natural supports to develop and friendships to evolve. Understanding the delicate nature of social situations among students and having the ability to fade from the scene whenever possible allow for these relationships to grow.

Paraprofessionals also demonstrate a leadership role when they create positive and reinforcing environments for students. This increases learning and performance among students and creates a school community in which students feel connected. Other staff members who may be unfamiliar with the student learn by observing how the paraprofessional uses effective communication strategies.

Record Keeping   School and district procedures may require documentation of contact time for paraprofessionals assisting students with disabilities. Logs or time sheets should be current and accurate at all times.

The following example illustrates a classroom that uses a range of personal supports, along with curricular and technological supports.

Welcome to Sojourner Truth Middle School

Ms. Patel's seventh-grade environmental science class is in the midst of an investigation. Her students are exploring an essential question: "Who is the earth for?" (Jorgensen, 1998). Earlier this morning, in their language arts class, they discussed the concept of leavers and takers in an environment, a debate featured in the book Ishmael *(Quinn, 1992). Then, they attended Ms. Chang's world civilizations class, where they are studying ancient Greece and participated in a Socratic dialogue on the role of humans as keepers of the planet. The students have become familiar with Socratic dialogue because* Ishmael *is written in this format. This after-*

noon, they will be engaged in a research lab on endangered species. Previously, students have been organized into a village (whole class), clans (groups of 12), and lodges (groups of 4). Ms. Patel has used heterogeneous groupings to maximize participation and community building (Lapp et al., 1999). Today, each lodge is completing a research lab. They will use resources from the classroom and school media center to determine the characteristics of their assigned animal or plant and its territory, the conditions it needs to thrive, and what outside forces are threatening its continued survival. Tomorrow, the lodges will meet as clans to share their findings. The clans will assemble as a village to participate in a discussion that will lead to a village plan of action. Ms. Patel and Mr. Estes, the language arts teacher, will collaborate on the design of the village's plan of action so that most of the writing will be completed in his class.

The seventh-grade team that Ms. Patel leads often designs interdisciplinary units of instruction because it produces a deeper understanding of concepts for students (Jacobs, 1997). There are added benefits as well. At a previous team meeting, Mr. Estes noted, "These thematic lessons we've been using have really made a difference in the quality of accommodations and modifications. They seem more sensible." Mrs. Thibodeau, the special educator assigned to the seventh-grade team, nods in agreement. The team's focus on problem-based learning and an interdisciplinary approach has made her instructional and assessment duties more meaningful. Now, she has time to supervise and train the instructional aides assigned to the seventh grade. Because Sojourner Truth Middle School (STMS) has redefined roles and responsibilities for all staff, Mrs. Thibodeau works with both special education and Title I aides. The team has been pleasantly surprised at the impact this has had on their classes. Because adults are no longer exclusively assigned to students with particular disabilities, assistance is available for all members of the class.

Three students in Ms. Patel's third-period class illustrate the range of supports available to students at STMS. Victor is an active 12-year-old, who is interested in video games, football, and socializing with friends. He has a learning disability that affects his ability to comprehend text. Apri just turned 13 years old last month. She enjoys sharing her Backstreet Boys music collection with her friends. Apri has a significant cognitive disability and uses a power wheelchair and a Talk Back augmentative communication device. Jiri, also 13 years old, is the resident expert on the animal collection in Ms. Patel's classroom. His peers admire his skateboarding ability. He does not qualify for any categorical program because he does not have any identified disabilities.

Today, Victor's group, the Sky Lodge, is evaluating the status of the bald eagle, which is on the threatened species list. After the village receives instruction on what to investigate, Victor's group heads for the media center. Mr. Rawlings, a paraprofessional, will be accompanying them. Mrs. Thibodeau previously provided Victor with a blank graphic organizer featuring the questions that Ms. Patel had posed in class. Mr. Rawlings will assist Victor in completing the organizer by modeling the notetaking, then fading prompts. Mrs. Thibodeau trained the paraprofessional staff in this instructional strategy last month. Of course, the paraprofessional also is available to assist other members of the sky lodge. This part-time support is scheduled each Tuesday, when Ms. Patel's class does research.

The river lodge, led by Apri, will be researching the Chilean sea bass, an ocean fish recently added to the endangered species list. Because Mrs. Thibodeau collaborates with Ms. Patel using the unit lesson plan (see Chapter 3), she knows in advance which animal is assigned to the River Lodge. Because Apri's family speaks Portuguese at home, the special education teacher also collaborates with the teacher for assistance in programming her communication device with both Portuguese and English phrases. For this assignment, Mrs. Thibodeau created a graphic organizer with BoardMaker picture symbols that contain text from both languages. Her group has enjoyed learning vocabulary in two languages. Apri's support for today's activity comes primarily from her peers, who are learning to prompt her to use her communication device. Her orientation and mobility specialist uses the Tuesday trips to the media center to instruct Apri on navigating the school. Jack, an eighth-grader enrolled in the peer tutoring class, accompanies Apri to the media center to assist in using her Talk Back. He is a technology whiz and has become proficient at programming her communication device to keep up with the demands of the conversation. Today, Apri is using natural support (her lodge mates), supplemental support (her orientation and mobility specialist), and peer tutoring support.

Jiri's Mesa Lodge is gathering information on the Florida panther. They are surprised to learn that fewer than 50 remain, mostly in remote regions of the Everglades. A heated discussion breaks out between Jiri and a lodge mate over whether alligators or crocodiles live in the Everglades, and Jiri raises his voice and curses. The special educator is circulating in the media center to assist students (specialized support) and overhears the ruckus. She is able to intervene immediately and facilitate a resolution between the two students. She makes a written note of the incident because she has witnessed three other conflicts with Jiri in the past few weeks. She will add Jiri to the agenda at next week's team meeting and ask the other teachers whether they have made similar observations. The team may ask her for guidance in conducting a functional behavioral assessment (O'Neill et al., 1994). Today, Jiri, a general educa-

tion student, benefited from the incidental support available in the media center. Mrs. Thibodeau serves as a consultant to the rest of the team on positive behavior supports and interventions (see Chapter 8). They have been able to refine their classroom management this year because of her input.

The seventh-grade team at STMS takes pride in its multilevel instructional practice and its connection to authentic assessments (Jacobs, 1997; Tomlinson, 1995). Using the unit lesson plan, Mrs. Thibodeau knows that the students will be assessed on several projects. Students have kept a reflective log, and Mr. Estes, Ms. Chang, and Ms. Patel have read and responded to the entries throughout the unit. Victor uses a word processing program on the computer to take advantage of the editing, spell check, and word prediction features. Apri uses magazine pictures to create a picture response to the writing prompts and is assisted in the placement of the pictures by Mr. Rawlings (intermittent support). These accommodations and modifications were featured in their student profiles and were designed by the special education teacher (specialized support). Although Jiri required no accommodations to this assessment, he took advantage of the graphic organizer used by Victor to plan some of his compositions.

A culminating project was used to assess student progress. Each lodge created an oral and written report to answer the essential question, "Who is the earth for?" Each group met with one of the teachers to propose a project. Apri's group chose to write a court drama, with the takers as the defendant and the leavers as the plaintiff. Apri's lines were programmed into her communication device. Most of the students in the class, including Jiri and Victor, were assessed using an eight-point rubric (see Chapter 6) constructed by the class and Ms. Chang. Apri was assessed using an individualized, four-point rubric (see Chapter 6). Mrs. Thibodeau and the seventh-grade team gave Apri a collaborative grade for her project, based on her mastery of the content for which she was responsible and progress toward her IEP goals, as outlined in her infused skills grid (specialized support). When the team met to debrief on the unit, they agreed it was a success. Ms.Chang made some suggestions about how she might refine the rubric creation process, and Mr. Estes shared the documented progress that several students made in their writing skills. Mrs. Thibodeau made notes on the success of the accommodations and modifications created for the students with IEPs. Mr. Rawlings, the paraprofessional, had been an important informant. The seventh-grade team agreed on a major point—the curriculum design of the unit allowed for a wide range of diverse learners to participate in a meaningful way. Ms. Patel said, "I was really hesitant about whether weekly research sessions would work. After all, it means I've got students spread out all over the school. But it really works because we can put adults where we need them, when we need them."

After the meeting was over, Mrs. Thibodeau took a copy of the unit lesson plan and samples of adapted assignments to be filed in the seventh-grade curriculum bank. This bank was created last year by the principal, Ms. Kirby, to serve as a central source for all teachers in the school. Just last week, Mr. Redstone, a new social studies teacher, told Ms. Kirby, "I've never worked in a school before where I felt I could step into my teaching assignment so well prepared. Using the curriculum bank gave me great ideas on how to teach my units." Mrs. Thibodeau also depends on the curriculum bank as a way to record the accommodations and modifications made for students, a real boon when talking with families. This year, Ms. Kirby has required the use of the unit lesson plan to gain access to curricular, technology, and personal supports for students at STMS. The consistent use of communication procedures has resulted in timely and effective delivery of compensatory education services. Ms. Kirby is fond of saying, "No one is going to give us more resources, so we've got to use the resources we have in a smarter way." In addition to the AULP, two other tools are used at the school to streamline the information flow. The infused skills grid (see Chapter 4) and student profile ensure that general education teachers have been provided with important information developed in a student's IEP meeting. Their format serves as a summary of the goals and services detailed on the IEP, not as a replacement of the requirement to provide teachers with copies of the IEP.

THE STUDENT PROFILE:
A COMMUNICATION TOOL FOR TEACHERS

A key factor in the success of providing educational services to students is the ability to communicate effectively with general education teachers about students' academic and personal support needs, lesson planning, and input to IEPs. Several processes have been developed to increase communication among teachers, including the infused skills grid and AULP. Let's look at a third tool in the communication process: the student profile.

This profile, provided to general education teachers at the beginning of each term, outlines an individual student's needs and classroom considerations for that student (see Figure 9.1). This document should be created by family members, teachers, and others who are close to the student and should reflect many of the decisions and strategies developed by the IEP committee. Specifically, this form contains the following information:

Name: _____ Grade: _____ Student number: _____

Parent/Guardian: _____ Telephone number: _____

Class Schedule:

Quarter: _____ Block 1: _____ Room ____

Block 2: _____ Room ____

Block 3: _____ Room ____

Block 4: _____ Room ____

Block 5: _____ Room ____

Advocate teacher:

Specific objectives for this class:

Areas of strengths/interests:

Successful learning strategies/modifications/adaptations needed:

Communication strategies:

Positive behavior support strategies:

Grading accommodations:

Important family/health information:

Figure 9.1. Blank student profile.

- Specific objectives for the class: The specific objectives often are taken from the IEP but written in accessible language for teachers.
- Areas of strengths and interests: A teacher may be able to use this information when designing projects or class activities.
- Successful learning strategies, modifications, and adaptations needed: This section of the form is useful for describing strategies as well as successful curriculum modifications.
- Communication strategies: This section includes any type of augmentative or alternative communication supports that have been developed.
- Positive behavior support strategies: Helpful hints about behavior supports are important for teachers, especially if these strategies have been successful in the past.
- Grading accommodations: Students may require additional time on tests, oral versions of the test, or alternatives to the test.
- Important family and health information: Additional health information useful for teachers can be recorded in this section.

Apri's student profile for this term appears in Figure 9.2. Mrs. Thibodeau completed the profile and reviewed it with the general education teachers before the term began. They were relieved to see that many of their questions already had been addressed, especially regarding communication and behavior. She also made note of questions that she had not addressed on the form, such as Apri's use of pictures to support her written work. She later said, "I was reminded once again by their questions just how important it is that we have time to share information. Sometimes we forget that the information we're carrying in our heads isn't available to everyone." Mr. Estes jokingly remarked that the team could use a student profile for each of the seventh-graders!

The coordination of personal supports allows all the other supports to happen—behavioral, technological, and curricular. These supports are sophisticated and varied in the way they are used in an inclusive school. These specialized and natural supports include special educators, general educators, paraprofessionals, and peers. The challenge for educators and administrators is to create flexible and responsive systems that wisely use these supports. This means that many procedures that have been in place because "that's the way we've always done it" must be reexamined through an inclusive lens. Mobilizing personal supports can create the safety net so many need, yet to which so few can gain access. Extending what we know about effective support to make it available to all is, as the principal, Ms. Kirby says, a way to "use resources in a smarter way."

Name: _Apri Perreira_   Grade: _7_   Student number: _1025_

Parent/Guardian: _Miguel and Sonia Perreira_   Telephone number: _555-6543_

Class Schedule:

Quarter: ____1____   Block 1: _Language Arts_   Room _246_

                 Block 2: _World Civilizations_   Room _251_

                 Block 3: _3-D Art_   Room _117_

                 Block 4: _Environmental Science_   Room _249_

                 Block 5: _Pre-algebra_   Room _248_

Advocate teacher: _Marie Thibodeau_

Specific objectives for this class: _Manage personal belongings, use a communication device to make choices, work in small groups to complete long-range academic tasks, travel throughout the school campus, utilize a visual schedule, complete assignments, and participate in conversations with peers and adults._

Areas of strengths/interests: _Apri is friendly and outgoing. She has an extensive collection of popular music CDs, and enjoys listening to them with peers. She listens intently to books on tape and read-alouds. Apri also is skilled at participating in small-group activities._

Successful learning strategies/modifications/adaptations needed: _Apri needs to have topical picture symbols and magazine photos available to support her written responses. Written tests and assignments are modified to reduce the number and type of items. She uses books on tape to complete reading assignments. Her communication device needs to be programmed to reflect current content-area vocabulary. She uses a notetaker to record responses and written assignments._

Communication strategies: _Apri uses a Talk Back augmentative communication device. She also makes choices using BoardMaker symbols. Apri uses a daily picture schedule that should be reviewed with her before she makes a transition to another activity or class. Be sure to speak to Apri directly and not to the support person assisting her. When addressing her, position yourself in her visual field._

Positive behavior support strategies: _Apri benefits from the consistent use of her picture schedule, especially before changes in activity. She also needs opportunities to learn how to make choices in a manner others can respond to. Apri is currently working on requesting breaks, and her requests should be consistently honored._

Grading accommodations: _The special education teacher and content-area teacher issue collaborative grades for April's assignments. For semester grades, each teacher grades her on 1) mastery of content she is responsible for, and 2) her progress toward IEP goals (see "Specific objectives for this class"). These grades are averaged to yield a collaborative report card grade._

Important family/health information: _Apri's home language is Portuguese, and her family feels more comfortable communicating with assistance from an interpreter. Mr. Sandomenico from our staff provides this service. Apri is allergic to peanut butter._

Figure 9.2.   Student profile for Apri.

Educators are all too aware of the complex societal forces that buffet today's students. Consider the author of the following poem—a seventh-grade special education student attending a large, urban school:

I am . . . a clown
I wonder if I can change
I hear laughing
I see happy faces
I want to be like them
I am very sad
I pretend I am changed
I feel very sad
I touch my heart
I worry I will be like this all the time
I cry in my heart
I am a sad clown
I understand where I was wrong
I say I laugh too much
I dream of changing
I try to change
Someday I hope my dream comes true
I am a sad clown

References

Alexander, W.M., & George, P.S. (1981). *The exemplary middle school*. New York: Holt, Rhinehart & Winston.

Americans with Disabilities Act (ADA) of 1990, PL 101-336, 42 U.S.C. §§ 12101 *et seq.*

Ames, N.L., & Miller, E. (1994). *Changing middle schools: How to make schools work for young adolescents*. San Francisco: Jossey-Bass.

Andreasen, A. (1995). *Marketing social change: Changing behavior to promote health, social development, and the environment*. San Francisco: Jossey-Bass.

Anson, D.K. (1997). *Alternative computer access: A guide to selection*. Philadelphia: F.A. Davis Co.

Apple, M.W., & Beane, J.A. (1995). *Democratic schools*. Alexandria, VA: Association for Supervision and Curriculum Development (ASCD).

Arhar, J.M. (1992). Interdisciplinary teaming and the social bonding of middle level students. In J.L. Irvin (Ed.), *Transforming middle level education: Perspectives and possibilities* (pp. 139–161). Needham Heights, MA: Allyn & Bacon.

Arhar, J.M., Johnston, J.J., & Markle, G.C. (1988). The effects of teaming and other collaborative arrangements. *Middle School Journal, 19,* 22–25.

Arhar, J.M., Johnston, J.J., & Markle, G.C. (1989). The effects of teaming on students. *Middle School Journal, 20,* 24–27.

Assistive Technology Act of 1998, PL 105-394, 29 U.S.C. §§ 3001 *et seq.*

Atkins, B. (1995). Diversity: A continuing rehabilitation challenge and opportunity. In S. Walker, K.A. Turner, M. Haile-Michael, A. Vincent, & M.D. Miles (Eds.), *Disability and diversity: New leadership for a new era* (pp. 34–36). Washington, DC: Howard University.

Baer, D.M. (1993). Commentary: Policy and procedure, as always. In R.A. Gable & S.F. Warren (Eds.), *Strategies for teaching students with mild to severe mental retardation* (pp. 269–277). Baltimore: Paul H. Brookes Publishing Co.

Beck, M. (1997). The assessment conundrum. In J. Flood, D. Lapp, & K. Wood (Eds.), *Staff development guide for middle school teachers* (pp. 211–215). New York: Macmillan/McGraw-Hill.

Berends, M., & King, M.B. (1994). A description of restructuring in nationally nominated schools: Legacy of the iron cage? *Educational Policy, 18,* 28–50.

Biklen, D. (1992). *Schooling without labels: Parents, educators, and inclusive education*. Philadelphia: Temple.

Bishop, C.H. (1952). *Twenty and ten*. New York: Penguin.

Bonstignl, J.J. (1992). *Schools of quality: An introduction to total quality management in education*. Alexandria, VA: Association for Supervision and Curriculum Development (ASCD).

Brooks, J.G., & Brooks, M.G. (1993). *The case for constructivist classrooms*. Alexandria, VA: Association for Supervision and Curriculum Development (ASCD).

Brown v. Board of Educ., 347 U.S. 483 (1954).

Brown, L., Ford, A., Nisbet, J., Sweet, M., Donnellan, A., & Gruenewald, L. (1983). Opportunities available when severely handicapped students attend chronological age-appropriate regular schools. *Journal of The Association for Persons with Severe Handicaps, 8,* 16–24.

Brown, L., Long, E., Udvari-Solner, A., Davis, L., VanDeventer, P., Ahlgren, C., Johnson, F., & Gruenewald, L., & Jorgensen, J. (1989). The home school: Why students with severe intellectual disabilities must attend the schools of their brothers, sisters, friends, and neighbors. *Journal of The Association for Persons with Severe Handicaps, 14,* 1–7.

Brown, L., Schwarz, P., Udvari-Solner, A., Kampschroer, E., Johnson, F., Jorgensen, J., & Gruenewald, L. (1991). How much time should students with severe intellectual disabilities spend in the regular education classrooms and elsewhere? *Journal of The Association for Persons with Severe Handicaps, 16,* 39–47.

Buswell, B.E., & Schaffner, C.B. (1995). Resources for advancing inclusive education. In R.A. Villa & J.S. Thousand (Eds.), *Creating an inclusive school* (pp. 168–180). Alexandria, VA: Association for Supervision and Curriculum Development (ASCD).

Calabrese, R.L., & Seldin, C.A. (1987). A contextual analysis of alienation among school constituencies. *Urban Education, 22,* 1–7.

Carlson, R. (1996). *Reframing and reform: Perspectives on organization, leadership, and school change.* White Plains, NY: Longman.

Carnegie Council on Adolescent Development. (1989). *Turning points: Preparing American youth for the 21st Century.* New York: Carnegie Corporation.

Carr, E.G., Levin, L., McConnachie, G., Carlson, J.I., Kemp, D.C., & Smith, C.E. (1994). *Communication-based intervention for problem behavior: A user's guide for producing positive change.* Baltimore: Paul H. Brookes Publishing Co.

Castagnera, L., Fisher, D., Rodifer, K., & Sax, C. (1998). *Deciding what to teach and how to teach it: Connecting students through curriculum and instruction.* Colorado Springs, CO: PEAK Parent Center.

Certo, N., Pumpian, I., Fisher, D., Storey, K., & Smalley, K. (1997). Focusing on the point of transition: A service integration model. *Education and Treatment of Children, 20,* 68–84.

Clark, S.N., & Clark, D.C. (1992). The pontoon transitional design: A missing link in research on interdisciplinary teaming. *Research in Middle Level Education, 15,* 57–81.

Clark, S.N., & Clark, D.C. (1994). *Restructuring the middle level school: Implications for school leaders.* Albany: State University of New York Press.

Cohen, E. (1981). Sociology looks at team teaching. *Research in Sociology of Education and Educational Socialization, 2,* 163–193.

Coleman, J.S. (1990). *Foundations of social theory.* Cambridge, MA: Harvard University Press.

Cushing, L.S., & Kennedy, C. (1997). Academic effects on students without disabilities who serve as peer supports for students with disabilities in general education classrooms. *Journal of Applied Behavioral Analysis, 30,* 139–152.

Damico, S.B., Bell, N., & Green, C. (1981). Effects of school organizational structure on interracial friendships in middle schools. *Journal of Educational Research, 74,* 388–393.

Danielson, L.C., & Bellamy, G.T. (1989). State variation in the placement of children with handicaps in segregated environments. *Exceptional Children, 55,* 448–455.

Delpit, L. (1995). *Other people's children: Cultural conflict in the classroom.* New York: New Press.

Dryfoos, J.G. (1994). *Full-service schools: A revolution in health and social services for children, youth, and families.* San Francisco: Jossey-Bass.

Dunlap, G., & Kern, L. (1993). Assessment and intervention for children within the instructional curriculum. In J. Reichle & D.P. Wacker (Eds.), *Communicative alternatives to challenging behavior: Integrating functional assessment and intervention strategies* (pp. 177–204). Baltimore: Paul H. Brookes Publishing Co.

Eastmond, D.V. (1992). Effective facilitation of computer conferencing. *Continuing Higher Education Review, 56*, 155–167.

Education for All Handicapped Children Act of 1975, PL 94-142, 20 U.S.C. §§ 1400 *et seq.*

Elmore, R.F. (1980). Backward mapping: Implementation research and policy decisions. *Political Science Quarterly, 94*, 601–616.

Epstein, J.L., & Mac Iver, D. (1990). *Education in the middle grades: National practices and trends.* Columbus, OH: National Middle School Association.

Espinosa, R., & Ochoa, A. (1992, Spring). *The educational attainment of California youth: A public equity crisis.* San Diego, CA: Multifunctional Resource Center.

Fatemi, E. (1999, September 23). Building the digital curriculum. *Education Week,* 5–11.

Feinberg, W., & Soltis, J.F. (1992). *School and society.* New York: Teachers College Press.

Figueroa, R., & Garcia, E. (1994). Issues in testing students from culturally and linguistically diverse backgrounds. *Multicultural Education, 2*(1), 10–19.

Fisher, D. (1996). *Organizational climate, typical student attitudes, and parent satisfaction: A study of a traditional and an inclusive high school.* Unpublished doctoral dissertation, San Diego State University and Claremont Graduate School, California.

Fisher, D., Roach, V., & Kearns, J. (1998). Statewide assessment systems: Who's in and who's out? *CISP Issue Brief, 3*(1), 1–7.

Fisher, D., Sax, C., & Jorgensen, C. (1998). Philosophical foundations of inclusive, restructuring schools. In C. Jorgensen (Ed.), *Restructuring high schools to include all students* (pp. 29–47). Baltimore: Paul H. Brookes Publishing Co.

Fisher, D., Sax, C., & Pumpian, I. (1996). From intrusion to inclusion: Myths and realities in our schools. *The Reading Teacher, 49*, 580–584.

Fisher, D., Sax, C., & Pumpian, I. (Eds.). (1999). *Inclusive high schools: Learning from contemporary classrooms.* Baltimore: Paul H. Brookes Publishing Co.

Fisher, D., Sax, C., Pumpian, I., Rodifer, K., & Kreikemeirer, P. (1997). Including all students in the high school reform agenda. *Education and Treatment of Children, 20*, 59–67.

Flood, J., Lapp, D., & Wood, K.D. (1997). *Staff development guide.* New York: Macmillan/McGraw-Hill.

Florini, B. (1989). Teaching styles and technology. In E.R. Hayes (Ed.), *Effective teaching styles: New directions for adult and continuing education* (pp. 41–53). San Francisco: Jossey-Bass.

Ford, A., Davern, L., & Schnorr, R. (1991). Inclusive education: "Making sense" of the curriculum. In S. Stainback & W. Stainback (Eds.), *Curriculum considerations in inclusive classrooms: Facilitating learning for all students* (pp. 37–64). Baltimore: Paul H. Brookes Publishing Co.

Fraser, S. (Ed.). (1995). *The bell curve wars: Race, intelligence, and the future of America.* New York: Basic Books.

Fuchs, D., & Fuchs, L. (1995). Sometimes separate is better. *Educational Leadership, 52*(4), 22–26.

Fuhrman, S. (Ed.). (1993). *Designing coherent education policy.* San Francisco: Jossey-Bass.

Fullan, M. (1993). *Change forces.* London: Falmer.

Fullan, M., & Hargreaves, A. (1996). *What's worth fighting for in your school?* New York: Teachers College Press.

Galvin, J.C., & Scherer, M.J. (1996). *Evaluating, selecting, and using appropriate assistive technology.* Gaithersburg, MD: Aspen.

Gambrell, L.B., Morrow, L.M., Neuman, S.B., & Pressley, M. (1999). *Best practices in literacy instruction.* New York: Guilford.

George, P., & Oldaker, L. (1985). *Evidence for the middle school.* Columbus, OH: National Middle School Association.

George, P., & Shewey, K. (1994). *New evidence for the middle school.* Columbus, OH: National Middle School Association.

Giangreco, M.F., Edelman, S.W., Luiselli, T.E., & MacFarland, S.Z.C. (1997). Helping or hovering? Effects of instructional assistant proximity on students with disabilities. *Exceptional Children, 64,* 7–18.

Gilbert, T.F. (1981–1982). Human incompetence: The autobiography of an educational revolutionist. *Journal of Organizational Behavior Management, 3,* 55–67.

Goals 2000: Educate America Act of 1994, PL 103-227, 20 U.S.C. §§ 5801 *et seq.*

Goldiamond, I. (1974). Toward a constructional approach to social problems. *Behaviorism, 2,* 1–84.

Goldiamond, I. (August, 1992). *Nonlinear analysis.* Invited address given at the annual conference of the American Psychological Association, Los Angeles.

Goodlad, J. (1984). *A place called school.* New York: McGraw-Hill.

Haberman, M. (1991). The pedagogy of poverty versus good teaching. *Phi Delta Kappan, 73*(4), 290–294.

Helmstetter, E., Peck, C.A., & Giangreco, M.F. (1994). Outcomes of interactions with peers with moderate or severe disabilities: A statewide survey of high school students. *Journal of The Association for Persons with Severe Handicaps, 19,* 263–276.

Herrnstein, R.J., & Murray, C. (1994). *The bell curve: Intelligence and class structure in American life.* New York: Free Press.

Hill, H. (1995). Ideas and programs to assist in the untracking of American schools. In H. Pool & J.A. Page (Eds.), *Beyond tracking: Finding success in inclusive schools* (pp. 105–116). Bloomington, IN: Phi Delta Kappa.

Hoestlandt, J. (1993). *Star of fear, star of hope.* New York: Walker.

Horner, R.H., & Carr, E.G. (1997). Behavioral support for students with severe disabilities: Functional assessment and comprehensive intervention. *Journal of Special Education, 31,* 84–104.

Hoy, W.K., & Sabo, D.J. (1997). *Quality middle schools: Open and healthy.* Thousand Oaks, CA: Sage.

Individuals with Disabilities Education Act (IDEA) of 1990, PL 101-476, 20 U.S.C. §§ 1400 *et seq.*

Individuals with Disabilities Education Act (IDEA) Amendments of 1997, PL 105-17, 20 U.S.C. §§ 1400 *et seq.*

Irvin, J.L. (1992). *Transforming middle level education: Perspectives and possibilities.* Needham Heights, MA: Allyn & Bacon.

Irvin, J.L. (1997). *What current research says to the middle level practitioner.* Columbus, OH: National Middle School Association.

Jacobs, H.H. (1989). *Interdisciplinary curriculum: Design and implementation.* Alexandria, VA: Association for Supervision and Curriculum Development (ASCD).

Jacobs, H.H. (1997). *Mapping the big picture: Integrating curriculum and assessment K–12*. Alexandria, VA: Association for Supervision and Curriculum Development (ASCD).

Janus, P.L. (1994). The role of school administration. In R.C. Savage & G.F. Wolcott (Eds.), *Educational dimensions of acquired brain injury* (pp. 475–487). Austin, TX: PRO-ED.

Johnson, D.W., Johnson, R.T., & Holubec, E.J. (1986). *Circles of learning: Cooperation in the classroom*. Edina, MN: Interaction.

Jorgensen, C.M. (Ed.). (1998). *Restructuring high schools for all students*. Baltimore: Paul H. Brookes Publishing Co.

Kendall, J.S., & Marzano, R.J. (1997). *Content knowledge: A compendium of standards and benchmarks for K–12 education* (2nd ed.). Aurora, CO: McREL.

Kennedy, C.H., Horner, R.H., & Newton, J.S. (1989). Social contacts of adults with severe disabilities living in the community: A descriptive analysis of relationship patterns. *Journal of The Association for Persons with Severe Handicaps, 14*, 190–196.

Kennedy, C.H., Jolivette, K., Long, T., Cox, J., Tang, J.C., & Thompson, T. (2000). *Effects of a comprehensive schoolwide positive behavior support system for students with behavioral challenges*. Manuscript submitted for publication.

Kennedy, C.H., Shukla, S., & Fryxell, D. (1997). Comparing the effects of educational placement on the social relationships of intermediate school students with severe disabilities. *Exceptional Children, 64*, 31–47.

Kennedy, C.H., & Thompson, T. (2000). Health conditions contributing to problem behavior among people with mental retardation and developmental disabilities. In M. Wehmeyer & J. Patten (Eds.), *Mental retardation in the 21st century* (pp. 211–231). Austin, TX: PRO-ED.

Kerr, J. (1971). *When Hitler stole pink rabbit*. New York: Bantam Doubleday Dell.

Klecker, B.M., & Loadman, W.E. (1999). Measuring principals' openness to change on three dimensions: Affective, cognitive and behavioral. *Journal of Instructional Psychology, 26*, 213–225.

Kleinert, H.L., Kearns, J.F., & Kennedy, S. (1997). Accountability for all students: Kentucky's alternative portfolio assessment for students with moderate and severe cognitive disabilities. *Journal of The Association for Persons with Severe Handicaps, 22*, 88–101.

Kozol, J. (1991). *Savage inequalities*. New York: Crown.

Kyle, R.M.J. (1995). *School-to-work transition and its role in the systemic reform of education: The experience of Jefferson County, Kentucky, and the Kentucky Education Reform Act*. Washington, DC: Academy for Educational Development.

Langland, S., Lewis-Palmer, T., & Sugai, G. (1998). Teaching respect in the classroom: An instructional approach. *Journal of Behavioral Education, 8*, 245–262.

Lapp, D., Fisher, D., & Flood, J. (1999). Does it matter how you're grouped for instruction? Yes! Flexible grouping patterns promote student learning. *The California Reader, 33*(1), 28–32.

Lau v. Nichols, 414 U.S. 563 (1974).

Lerner, J. (1993). *Learning disabilities: Theories, diagnosis and teaching strategies*. Boston: Houghton Mifflin.

Lichtenstein, S. (1993). Transition from school to adulthood: Case studies of adults with learning disabilities who dropped out of school. *Exceptional Children, 59*, 336–347.

Lieberman, A. (1990). *Schools as collaborative cultures: Creating the future now*. New York: Falmer Press.

Lieberman, A. (1995). *The work of restructuring schools: Building from the ground up*. New York: Teachers College Press.

Lindsley, O.R. (1991). Precision teaching's unique legacy from B. F. Skinner. *Journal of Behavioral Education, 1*, 253–266.

Linn, M.C., & Songer, M.B. (1991). Cognitive and conceptual change in adolescence. *American Journal of Education, 99*, 379–417.

Lipman, P. (1997). Restructuring in context: A case study of teacher participation and the dynamics of ideology, race, and power. *American Educational Research Journal, 34*, 3–37.

Little, J.W. (1982). Norms of collegiality and experimentation: Workplace conditions of school success. *American Educational Research Journal, 19*, 325–340.

Lounsbury, J.H. (1992). Perspectives on the middle school movement. In J.L. Irvin (Ed.), *Transforming middle level education: Perspectives and possibilities* (pp. 3–15). Needham Heights, MA: Allyn & Bacon.

Lovett, H. (1996). *Learning to listen: Positive approaches and people with difficult behavior*. Baltimore: Paul H. Brookes Publishing Co.

Lowry, L. (1989). *Number the stars*. New York: Bantam Doubleday Dell.

Lowry, L. (1993). *The giver*. New York: Bantam Doubleday Dell.

Luiselli, J.K., & Cameron, M.J. (1998). *Antecedent control: Innovative approaches to behavioral support*. Baltimore: Paul H. Brookes Publishing Co.

Lytle, J.H. (1992). Is special education serving minority students? A response to Singer and Butler. In T. Hehir & T. Latus (Eds.), *Special education at the century's end: Evolution of theory and practice since 1970* (pp. 191–196). Cambridge, MA: Harvard Educational Review.

Mac Iver, D.J. (1990). Meeting the needs of young adolescents: Advisory groups, interdisciplinary teaching teams, and school transition programs. *Phi Delta Kappan, 71*, 457–464.

Mace, R. (1998). Designing for the 21st century. [On-line]. Available: www.adaptenv.org/21century/1998_overview/plenary_speech_mace.htm

March, J.G., & Simon, H. (1993). *Organizations* (2nd ed.). Cambridge, MA: Blackwell.

Martin, K.M. (1999). Creating and nurturing strong teams. *Middle School Journal, 30*, 15–21.

Martusewicz, R.A., & Reynolds, W.M. (Eds.). (1994). *Inside out: Contemporary critical perspectives in education*. New York: St. Martin.

McDonnell, L.M., & McLaughlin, M.J. (1997). *Educating one and all: Students with disabilities and standards-based reform*. Washington, DC: National Academy Press.

McEwin, C.K., Dickinson, T.S., & Jenkins, D. (1995). *America's middle schools: Practices and progress—A 25 year perspective*. Columbus, OH: National Middle School Association.

McGregor, G., & Vogelsberg, R.T. (1998). *Inclusive schooling practices: Pedagogical and research foundations*. Pittsburgh: Allegheny University of the Health Sciences, Consortium on Inclusive Schooling Practices.

McLaughlin, M., Talbert, J., Kahne, J., & Powell, J. (1990). Constructing a personalized school environment. *Phi Delta Kappan, 72*, 230–235.

McPartland, J.M. (1987). *Balancing high quality subject-matter instruction with positive students-teacher relations in the middle grades*. (Report No. 15). Baltimore: Johns Hopkins University, Center for Research on Elementary and Middle School.

Meier, D. (1995). *The power of their ideas: Lessons for America from a small school in Harlem*. Boston: Beacon.

Merenbloom, E.Y. (1991). *The team process in the middle school* (2nd ed.). New York: Routlage and Keegan Paul.

Meyer, L.H., Park, H., Grenot-Scheyer, M., Schwartz, I., & Harry, B. (1998). *Making friends: The influences of culture and development.* Baltimore: Paul H. Brookes Publishing Co.

Midgley, C., & Edelin, K.C. (1998). Middle school reform and early adolescent well-being: The good news and the bad. *Educational Psychologist, 33,* 195–206.

Murphy, J., & Louis, K.S. (1999). *Handbook of research on educational administration.* Washington, DC: American Educational Research Association.

National Association of State Boards of Education (NASBE). (1992). *Winners all: A call for inclusive schools.* Report of the NASBE Study Group on Special Education. Washington, DC: Author.

National Association of State Boards of Education (NASBE). (1996). *What will it take? Standards-based education for all students.* Alexandria, VA: Author.

National Center for Educational Outcomes. (1994). *Guidelines for inclusion of students with disabilities in large-scale assessments.* Minneapolis, MN: Author.

Nieto, S. (1996). *Affirming diversity: The sociopolitical context of multicultural education* (2nd ed). White Plains, NY: Longman.

Oakes, J. (1985). *Keeping track: How schools structure inequality.* New Haven, CT: Yale University.

Oakes, J. (1992). Can tracking research inform practice? *Educational Researcher, 21*(4), 12–21.

Ogle, D. (1986). KWL: A teaching model that develops active reading of expository text. *The Reading Teacher, 30,* 364–370.

Ogle, D. (1996). Study techniques that ensure content area reading success. In D. Lapp, J. Flood, & N. Farnan (Eds.), *Content area reading and learning: Instructional strategies* (pp. 277–290). Needham Heights, MA: Allyn & Bacon.

Olsen, K. (1994). Have we made progress in fifteen years of evaluating the effectiveness of special education programs? *Special Services in the Schools, 9*(2), 21–37.

O'Neill, R.E., Horner, R.H., Albin, R., Storey, K., Sprague, J., & Newton, J.S. (1994). *Functional analysis of problem behavior: A practical assessment guide.* Pacific Grove, CA: Brooks/Cole.

Onosko, J.J., & Jorgensen, C.M. (1998). Unit and lesson planning in the inclusive classroom: Maximizing learning opportunities for all students. In C.M. Jorgensen (Ed.), *Restructuring high schools for all students* (pp. 71–105). Baltimore: Paul H. Brookes Publishing Co.

Paulsen, G. (1987). *Hatchet.* New York: Aladdin.

Pennsylvania Association for Retarded Citizens v. Commonwealth of Pennsylvania, 334 F. Supp. 1257 (1971).

Phillips, G. (1995). Creating a real group in a virtual world. *Interpersonal Computing and Technology: An Electronic Journal for the 21st Century, 3*(4), 42–56.

Pool, H., & Page, J.A. (1995). *Beyond tracking: Finding success in inclusive schools.* Bloomington, IN: Phi Delta Kappa.

Poplin, M., & Weeres, J. (1992). *Voices from the inside: A report on schooling from inside the classroom.* Claremont, CA: Institute for Education in Transformation.

Posner, G. (1995). *Analyzing the curriculum* (2nd ed.). New York: McGraw-Hill.

Pugach, M.C. (1995). On the failure of imagination in inclusive schooling. *The Journal of Special Education, 29,* 212–223.

Pulliam, J.D., & Van Patten, J. (1995). *History of education in America* (6th ed). Englewood Cliffs, NJ: Prentice-Hall.

Pumpian, I., Fisher, D., Certo, N., & Smalley, K. (1997). Changing jobs: An essential part of career development. *Mental Retardation, 35,* 39–48.

Quinn, D. (1992). *Ishmael*. New York: Bantam / Turner.

Rehabilitation Act of 1973, PL 93-112, 29 U.S.C. §§ 701 *et seq.*

Rehabilitation Act Amendments of 1992, PL 102-569, 29 U.S.C. §§ 701 *et seq.*

Reichle, J., & Wacker, D.P. (1993). *Communicative alternatives to challenging behavior: Integrating functional assessment and intervention strategies.* Baltimore: Paul H. Brookes Publishing Co.

Reiss, J. (1972). *The upstairs room.* New York: HarperCollins.

Repp, A.C., Felce, D., & Barton, L.E. (1988). Basing the treatment of stereotypic and self-injurious behaviors on hypotheses of their causes. *Journal of Applied Behavior Analysis, 21,* 281–289.

Reutzel, D.R. (1999). Organizing literacy instruction: Effective grouping strategies and organizational plans. In L.B. Gambrell, L.M. Morrow, S.B. Neuman, & M. Pressley (Eds.), *Best practices in literacy instruction* (pp. 271–291). New York: Guilford.

Roach, V. (1991). Special education: New questions in an era of reform. *The State Board Connection, 11*(6), 1–7.

Roach, V. (1995). *Winning ways: Creating inclusive schools, classrooms, and communities.* Alexandria, VA: National Association of State Boards of Education (NASBE).

Roach, V. (1999). Reflecting on the least restrictive environment policy: Curriculum, instruction, placement. Three legs of the achievement stool. In D. Fisher, C. Sax, & I. Pumpian (Eds.), *Inclusive high schools: Learning from contemporary classrooms* (pp. 145–156). Baltimore: Paul H. Brookes Publishing Co.

Roach, V., & Caruso, M. (1997). Policies promoting inclusion: A case for systemic reform. *Education and Treatment of Children, 20,* 105–121.

Rosenholtz, S. (1989). *Teachers workplace: A study of social organizations.* New York: Longman.

Rottier, J. (1990). *Implementing and improving teaming: A handbook for middle level leaders.* Columbus, OH: National Middle School Association.

Rutherford, P. (1998). *Instruction for all students.* Alexandria, VA: Just ASK Publications.

Ryndak, D.L., & Alper, S. (1996). *Curriculum content for students with moderate and severe disabilities in inclusive settings.* Needham Heights, MA: Allyn & Bacon.

Sailor, W. (1991). Special education in the restructured school. *Remedial and Special Education, 12,* 8–22.

Sailor, W. (1996). New structures and systems change for comprehensive positive behavioral support. In L.K. Koegel, R.L. Koegel, & G. Dunlap (Eds.), *Positive behavioral support: Including people with difficult behavior in the community* (pp. 163–206). Baltimore: Paul H. Brookes Publishing Co.

Sailor, W. (in press). *Inclusive education and school/community partnerships.* New York: Teachers College Press.

Sanders, M.G. (1996). Action teams in action: Interviews and observations in three schools in the Baltimore School-Family-Community Partnership Program. *Journal of Education for Students Placed at Risk, 1,* 249–262.

Sautter, R.C. (1994). Who are today's city kids? Beyond the "deficit model." *Cityschools, 1*(1), 6–10.

Sax, C., Fisher, D., & Pumpian, I. (1996). Outcomes for students with severe disabilities: Case studies on the use of assistive technology in inclusive classrooms. *Technology and Disability, 5,* 327–334.

Scherer, M.J. (1996). *Living in the state of stuck.* Cambridge, MA: Brookline.

Scotti, J.R., & Meyer, L.H. (1999). *Behavioral intervention: Principles, models, and practices.* Baltimore: Paul H. Brookes Publishing Co.

Sergiovanni, T.J. (1992). *Moral leadership: Getting to the heart of school improvement.* San Francisco: Jossey-Bass.

Shanker, A. (1995). Full inclusion is neither free nor appropriate. *Educational Leadership, 52*(4), 18–21.

Shapiro, J.P. (1993). *No pity: People with disabilities forging a new civil rights movement.* New York: Times.

Simeonsson, R.J., & Simeonsson, N.E. (1999). Designing community-based school health services for at-risk students. *Journal of Educational and Psychological Consultation, 10,* 215–228.

Sizer, T. (1992). *Horace's school: Redesigning the American high school.* Boston: Houghton Mifflin.

Skrtic, T.M. (1995). *Disability and democracy: Reconstructing (special) education for postmodernity.* New York: Teachers College Press.

Sleeter, C.E. (1996). *Multicultural education as social activism.* Albany: State University of New York.

Sowell, T. (1994). Ethnicity and IQ. In S. Fraser (Ed.), *The bell curve wars: Race, intelligence, and the future of America* (pp. 70–79). New York: Basic Books.

Sprague, J., Sugai, G., & Walker, H. (1998). Antisocial behavior in schools. In T.S. Watson & F.M. Gresham (Eds.), *Handbook of child behavior therapy* (pp. 451–474). New York: Plenum Press.

Strom, R., & Strom, S. (1999). Establishing school volunteer programs. *Child and Youth Services, 20,* 175–188.

Swartz, J.L., & Martin, W.E. (1997). *Applied ecological psychology for schools within communities: Assessment and intervention.* Mahwah, NJ: Lawrence Erlbaum Associates.

Talley, R.C., & Schrag, J.A. (1999). Legal and public policy foundations supporting service integration for students with disabilities. *Journal of Educational and Psychological Consultation, 10,* 229–249.

Taylor, S.J. (1988). Caught in the continuum: A critical analysis of the principle of least restrictive environment. *Journal of The Association for Persons with Severe Handicaps, 13,* 41–53.

Technology-Related Assistance for Individuals with Disabilities Act of 1988, PL 100-407, 29 U.S.C. §§ 2201 *et seq.*

Thornburg, D.D. (1994). *Education in the communication age.* San Carlos, CA: Starsong.

Tomlinson, C.A. (1995). *How to differentiate instruction in mixed-ability groups.* Alexandria, VA: Association for Supervision and Curriculum Development (ASCD).

Trent, J.W. (1994). *Inventing the feeble mind: A history of mental retardation in the United States.* Berkeley: University of California Press.

Tucker, M.S., & Codding, J.B. (1998). *Standards for our schools: How to set them, measure them, and reach them.* San Francisco: Jossey-Bass.

U.S. Department of Education. (1994). *Changing education: Resources for systemic reform.* Washington, DC: Author.

U.S. Department of Education. (1996). *To assure the free appropriate public education of all children with disabilities: Eighteenth annual report to Congress.* Washington, DC: Author.

U.S. Department of Education, Office of Special Education Programs. (1993). *To assure the free appropriate public education of all children with disabilities: Fifteenth annual report to Congress on the implementation of the Individuals with Disabilities Education Act.* Washington, DC: Author.

Vandercook, T., York, J., & Forest, M. (1989). The McGill Action Planning System (MAPS): A strategy for building vision. *Journal of The Association for Persons with Severe Handicaps, 14,* 205–215.

Villa, R.A., & Thousand, J.S. (1992). How one district integrated special and general education. *Educational Leadership, 50,* 39–41.

Wagner, M. (1993). *The transition experiences of young people with disabilities. A summary of findings from the National Longitudinal Transition Study of Special Education Students* [ERIC Document Record # EC302815]. Menlo Park, CA: SRI.

Walker, H.M., Zeller, R.W., Close, D.W., Webber, J., & Gresham, F. (1999). The present unwrapped: Change and challenge in the field of behavior disorders. *Behavioral Disorders, 24,* 293–304.

Wang, M.C. (1997). Urban school reform: The next steps. *Education and Urban Society, 29*(3), 1–22.

Weiner, D.L., & Vining, A.R. (1992). *Policy analysis: Concepts and practice.* Englewood Cliffs, NJ: Prentice-Hall.

Wheelock, A. (1992). *Crossing the tracks: How untracking can save America's schools.* New York: New Press.

Whitaker, P., Barratt, P., Thomas, G., Potter, M., & Joy, H. (1998). Children with autism and peer group support: "Using circles of friends." *British Journal of Special Education, 25,* 60–64.

Wolfe, A. (1995). Has there been a cognitive revolution in America? The flawed sociology of *The Bell Curve.* In S. Fraser (Ed.), *The bell curve wars: Race, intelligence, and the future of America* (pp. 109–123). New York: Basic Books.

Wright, D.K. (1994). *A multicultural portrait of World War II.* New York: Marshall Cavendish.

Ziegler, S., & Mulhall, L. (1994). Establishing and evaluating a successful advisory program in a middle school. *Middle School Journal, 25,* 42–46.

Zigmond, N., & Baker, J.M. (1995). Concluding comments: Current and future practices in inclusive schooling. *Journal of Special Education, 29,* 245–250.

Index

Page references followed by *t* or *f* indicate tables or figures, respectively.

Ability grouping, 9
Accommodations, 53–55, 54*t*
  for specific students, 52–59
  for standardized achievement
    testing, 77, 78*t*
Accountability, 73–85
Achievement
  societal stereotypes of, 5–8
  structural variables that correlate
    with, 8–10
  technology to support, 89–103
Achievement testing, standardized,
  77, 78*t*
Activities
  class, 50–51
  learning experiences that link, 47
ADA, *see* Americans with Disabilities
    Act of 1990 (PL 101-336)
Adaptations
  high-tech, 91
  low-tech, 92–96
Administrative leadership, 17–26
Administrators
  commitment to inclusive education
    reform, 12–13
  practices to foster inclusion, 25
  support for best practices, 20–21
  support for innovation, 21
Advocacy, student, 35
Age appropriateness, 109, 110*t*
Aids
  to interpret test items, 77, 78*t*
  to respond to test items, 77, 78*t*
Alternative text formats, 64
Americans with Disabilities Act
    (ADA) of 1990 (PL 101-336),
    19, 90
Assessment(s), 51–52
  cloze, 80–82, 83*f*
  formal, 73–75, 74*t*
  functional, 108–112
  general educator role in, 125–127,
    126*t*

informal, 73–75, 74*t*–75*t*
  linking to accountability and
    instruction, 73–85
  multiple, 48
  paraprofessional role in, 128, 129*t*
  person-centered strategy, 97
  planning instruction with, 79–85
  for positive behavior support, 117
  purposes of, 75
  rationale for, 75–76
  self-evaluation sheets, 83, 84*f*
  special educator role in, 123, 124*t*
  standards and, 76
  statewide systems of, 76–79
Assessment information, 112–113
Assignments
  tiered, 68
  Weekly Assignment Sheets, 55–59,
    58*f*
Assistive technology
  web sites that offer resources,
    equipment, and services,
    101–102
  see also Technology
Assistive Technology Act (ATA) of
    1998 (PL 105-394), 90
ATA, *see* Assistive Technology Act of
    1998 (PL 105-394)

Backward mapping, 11
Behavior problems
  areas of particular relevance to, 109
  modeling appropriate behavior for,
    109, 111*t*
  patterns of, 113
  positive behavior support for,
    105–117
Belonging
  personal supports that lead to,
    119–138
  technology to support, 89–103
Best practices, 20

Best practices—*continued*
  checklist for Kaneohe Middle
    School, 39, 39*t*
  for classroom instruction, 109,
    110*t*–111*t*
  educational administrator support
    for, 20–21
Books, 50
  selecting, 63
Brown v. Board of Education, 6

CARS, *see* Center Activity Rotation
    System
Center Activity Rotation System
    (CARS), 69
Central unit issues, problems, or
    questions, 46–47
Changes, structural variables to, 10,
    11*t*
Character webs, 67
Choice, 109, 110*t*
Class activities, 50–51
Classroom
  best practices for, 109, 110*t*–111*t*
  examples, 92–96, 130–134
  influencing policy based on experi-
    ences in, 10–12
Cloze assessments of reading, 80–82,
    83*f*
  guidelines for, 82
Collaborative school teams, 27–40
Communication
  general educator role for, 126*t*, 127
  paraprofessional role for, 128–130,
    129*t*
  special educator role for, 123, 124*t*
Community
  school/community-based manage-
    ment, 22–24
  as variable to change, 10, 11*t*
Community volunteers, 24–25
Compacting, 65–66
Comprehension, cloze assessments
    of, 80–82, 83*f*
Computer access, 91
The Computer Accessibility
    Technology Packet, 71, 103
Concept maps, 67
Culminating projects, 48

Curriculum, 43
  core, 43–59
  elements of, 45–48
  example of supports, 130–134
  inclusive, 41–85
  integration of, 34
  meaningful and functional, 109,
    110*t*
  overlapping, 55
  streamlining, 54
  as variable to change, 10, 11*t*
Curriculum design, 53–55, 54*t*

Daily routines, 55, 56*f*
Dedicated reading time, 63–64
Differentiated instruction, 53–55, 54*t*,
    61–71
Differentiating instruction, 65
Disabilities, students with
  continuum of supports for, 52
  participation in standards-based
    lessons, 52–59
  participation in statewide assess-
    ment systems, 76–79
  standards-based reform and,
    44–45
Diversity
  differentiated instruction for di-
    verse students, 61–71
  promoting, 37

EASI project, *see* Equal Access to
    Software and Information
    project
Education
  contemporary problems and possi-
    bilities, 1–13
  higher education model, 29, 29*f*
  inclusive
    district commitment to, 12–13
    promoting, 3, 4
  structural variables that correlate
    with student achievement,
    8–10
  see also Schools
Education for All Handicapped
    Children Act of 1975
    (PL 94-142), 2, 19, 20

Educational administrators
  practices to foster inclusion, 25
  support for best practices, 20–21
  support for innovation, 21
Educational policy, 19–20
Educational roles, 122–134
Educational standards, 44
Educational technology
  guide for purchasing, 99
  see also Technology
ELD/ELL, *see* English Language
      Development for English
      Language Learners
Employability, 10, 11*t*
English Language Development for
      English Language Learners
      (ELD/ELL), 120
Environment, learning, 28
  small, 35–36
Equal Access to Software and
      Information (EASI) project, 71,
      102
Equipment
  web sites that offer, 101–102
  see also Technology
Ergonomics, 98
Evaluation
  self-evaluation sheets, 83, 84*f*
  see also Assessment(s)
Expression, modes of, 48

Final projects, 51–52
Flexible grouping, 69–70
Functional assessments, 108–112
Functional skills, 55, 56*f*

General educator, role of, 125–128,
      126*t*
Goal setting, 33–34
Goals 2000: Educate America Act of
      1994 (PL 103-227), 19
Grade levels as dimension of school
      teams, 32
Group learning strategies, 109, 111*t*
Grouping
  ability, 9
  flexible, 69–70
  interest groups, 66–67

Health care needs, special, 109, 111*t*
Higher education model, 29, 29*f*
Holistic writing rubrics, 79, 81*t*
Home–school partnerships, 39, 39*t*

IDEA, *see* Individuals with Disabili-
      ties Education Act of 1990
Inclusion
  fostering, 25–26
  implications of, 1
Inclusive education
  district commitment to, 12–13
  promoting, 3, 4
  lesson planning, 52, 53*f*
  middle school curriculum for,
      41–85
Inclusive schools
  general educator role in, 125–128,
      126*t*
  paraprofessional role in, 128–130,
      129*t*
  special educator role in, 122–125,
      124*t*
Independent projects, 66
Independent reading level, 82
Individuals with Disabilities
      Education Act (IDEA) of 1990
      (PL 101-476), 2, 90
Individuals with Disabilities
      Education Act (IDEA)
      Amendments of 1997
      (PL 105-17), 19, 90, 127
Information collection, 112
Information sources, 50
Infused skills grid, 55, 56*f*
Innovation, 21
Instruction
  best practices for, 109, 110*t*–111*t*
  classroom, 109, 110*t*–111*t*
  differentiated, 53–55, 54*t*, 61–71
  differentiating, 65
  elements of, 45–48
  general educator role in, 125, 126*t*
  linking assessment to, 73–85
  paraprofessional role in, 128, 129*t*
  planning, 79–85
  quality of, 39, 39*t*
  special educator role in, 122–123,
      124*t*

Instructional arrangements, 50
Instructional materials, 109, 110*t*
Instructional reading level, 82
Interdisciplinary team approach, 39,
    39*t*, 107–108
    student-based, 109, 111*t*
Interest groups, 66–67
Intermittent support, 120
Interview, structured, 109–112

Kaneohe Middle School
    best practices checklist for, 39, 39*t*
    example school team, 37–39
KWL (what do you KNOW, what
    do you WANT to know,
    and what did you LEARN)
    questions, 68

Lau v. Nichols, 6
Leadership
    administrative, 17–26
    general educator role in, 126*t*,
        127–128
    paraprofessional role in, 129*t*, 130
    of school teams, 33
    special educator role in, 123, 124*t*
Learning
    experiences that link, 47
    formats for, 48
    group learning strategies, 109, 111*t*
    via performance, 65
Learning environment, 28
    small, 35–36
Learning styles, 109, 111*t*
Lesson plans
    inclusive, 52, 53*f*
    sample science unit, 55, 57*f*
Lessons, standards-based, 49–52
    example, 49
    participation by students with dis-
        abilities, 52–59
Library visits, 62–63
Literacy, visual, 64

Mapping, backward, 11
Materials
    instructional, 109, 110*t*
    source, 47

Medications, 109, 111*t*
Membership, 119–138
    facilitating, 109, 110*t*
Middle school curriculum, *see*
    Curriculum
Middle school students, *see* Students
Middle schools, *see* Schools
Mission, 21–22
Missouri Technology Center for
    Special Education, 102
Modeling appropriate behavior, 109,
    111*t*
Modifications, 53–55, 54*t*
    for specific students, 52–59
Multiple assessments, 48

National Longitudinal Transition
    Study, 2
Natural supports, 119, 120, 121*t*
Neighborhood schools, 18

Objectives, infused, 55
Office of Special Education and
    Rehabilitative Services
    (OSERS), U.S. Department
    of Education, 99

Paraprofessional role, 128–130, 129*t*
Parent roles, 10, 11*t*
Part-time support, 120, 121*t*
Pedagogy
    ability grouping and, 9
    as variable to change, 10, 11*t*
Peer tutors, 120, 121*t*
*Pennsylvania Association for Retarded
    Citizens v. Commonwealth of
    Pennsylvania,* 6
Performance
    improved, 36–37
    as way to learn, 65
Person-centered assessment strategy,
    97
Personal supports, 119–138
    example classroom with, 130–134
Physical structure, 10, 11*t*
Placements, special, 9

Planning
  how teachers use assessments in,
    79–85
  times for, 33–34
  see also Lesson plans
Policy
  development of, 10–12
  educational, 19–20
  school district, 99–100
  successful strategies, 12
Positive behavior support, 105–117,
    109, 110*t*
  assessments for, 117
  definition of, 105–107
  development of strategies, 112–114
  important aspects of, 117
  information collection for, 112
  need for, 105
  structured interview for, 109–112
Practices, best, 20
  checklist for Kaneohe Middle
    School, 39, 39*t*
  for classroom instruction, 109,
    110*t*–111*t*
  educational administrator support
    for, 20–21
Problem behaviors
  areas of particular relevance to,
    109
  patterns of, 113
Professional development, 36
Projects, 50–51
  culminating, 48
  final, 51–52
  independent, 66
Public education, *see* Education;
    Schools
PL 93-112, *see* Rehabilitation Act of
    1973
PL 94-142, *see* Education for all
    Handicapped Children Act of
    1975
PL 100-407, *see* Technology-Related
    Assistance for Individuals
    with Disabilities Act of 1988
PL 101-336, *see* Americans with
    Disabilities Act (ADA) of 1990
PL 101-476, *see* Individuals with
    Disabilities Education Act
    (IDEA) of 1990

PL 102-569, *see* Rehabilitation Act
    Amendments of 1992
PL 103-227, *see* Goals 2000: Educate
    America Act of 1994
PL 105-17, *see* Individuals with
    Disabilities Education Act
    (IDEA) Amendments of 1997
PL 105-394, *see* Assistive Technology
    Act (ATA) of 1998

Questions, KWL (what do you
    KNOW, what do you WANT
    to know, and what did you
    LEARN), 68

Read alouds, 62
Reading
  cloze assessments of, 80–82, 83*f*
  frustration level, 82
  independent level, 82
  instructional level, 82
Reading time, 63–64
Record keeping
  general educator role in, 126*t*, 128
  paraprofessional role in, 129*t*, 130
  special educator role in, 123–125,
    124*t*
  student profiles, 134–138
Rehabilitation Act of 1973
    (PL 93-112), Section 504, 90
Rehabilitation Act Amendments
    of 1992 (PL 102-569),
    Section 508, 90
Resources, 102–103
  web sites, 101–102
Routines, 55, 56*f*
Rubrics, 79, 81*t*

Scheduling, 109, 110*t*
  dedicated reading time, 63–64
  flexible, 77, 78*t*
  infused skills grid for, 55, 56*f*
  planning times, 33–34
School climate, 39, 39*t*
School/community-based manage-
    ment, 22–24

School districts
   commitment to inclusive education
      reform, 12–13
   guide for purchasing educational
      technology, 99
   technology policies, responsibili-
      ties, and procedures, 99–100
School restructuring, 24
School structures, 15–40
   physical, 10, 11*t*
   with school teaming approach, 30*f*,
      30–31
   traditional, 29, 29*f*
School teams, 24, 29–31
   approach of, 30*f*, 30–31
   cautionary notes for, 37
   collaborative, 27–40
   example, Kaneohe Middle School,
      37–39, 39*t*
   function of, 31
   functional dimensions of, 33–35
   goal setting, 33–34
   importance of, 39–40
   interdepartmental composition of,
      31–33
   key components, 31–40
   leadership of, 33
   members
      appointment of, 32–33
      roles and responsibilities of, 33
      selection of, 32–33
      volunteer, 32–33
   model of, 30*f*, 30–31
   outcomes of, 35–39
   planning times for, 33–34
   structural dimensions of, 31–33
   structure of, 31
Schools
   home–school partnerships, 39,
      39*t*
   inclusive
      general educator role in,
         125–128, 126*t*
      paraprofessional role in,
         128–130, 129*t*
      special educator role in, 122–125,
         124*t*
   mission, 21–22
   neighborhood, 18

school teaming approach, 30*f*,
   30–31
vision, 21–22
Science, sample unit lesson plan for,
   55, 57*f*
Self-evaluation sheets, 83, 84*f*
Services
   assistive technology, 101–102
   special, 9
Skills
   infused skills grid, 55, 56*f*
   speaking checklist to track, 79, 80*t*
   types all students need to learn, 46
Smaller learning environments,
   35–36
Societal stereotypes, 5–8
Sojourner Truth Middle School
   (example classroom), 130–134
Source material, detailed, 47
Speaking checklist, 79, 80*t*
Special educator role, 122–125, 124*t*
Special health care needs, 109, 111*t*
Special placements, 9
Special services, 9
Specialized support staff, 120–122
Specialized supports, 119
Staff support
   natural, 120–122
   specialized, 120–122
   total, 120, 121*t*
Standardized achievement testing,
   accommodations for, 77, 78*t*
Standards
   and assessment, 76
   rationale for, 44
Standards-based lessons, 49–52
   example, 49
   participation by students with
      disabilities, 52–59
Standards-based reform, 44–45
Statewide assessment systems
   key questions for communication
      about, 77
   participation of students with
      disabilities in, 76–79
Stereotypes, societal, 5–8
Structured interview, 109–112
Student achievement
   societal stereotypes of, 5–8

structural variables that correlate
    with, 8–10
technology to support, 89–103
Student advocacy, 35
Student-based interdisciplinary
    teams, 109, 111t
Student participation, 39, 39t
Student profiles, 134–138
    components of, 134–136
    example, 136, 137f
    form, 134, 135f
Student progress
    improved performance, 36–37
    monitoring, 35
    multiple assessments of, 48
Student supports, 87–138
    levels of, 120, 121t
Students
    accommodations and modifica-
        tions for, 52–59
    with disabilities
        continuum of supports for, 52
        participation in standards-based
            lessons, 52–59
        participation in statewide assess-
            ment systems, 76–79
        standards-based reform and,
            44–45
    diverse, 61–71
    focus on, 109, 111t
    proportional representation of, 32
    roles of, 10, 11t
    teacher-to-student ratios, 32
Support(s)
    continuum of, 52
    example classroom with, 130–134
    for inclusive lesson planning, 52, 53f
    intermittent, 120, 121t
    levels of, 120, 121t
    natural, 119, 120, 121t
    part-time, 120, 121t
    personal, 119–138
    positive behavior, 105–117
    specialized, 119
    student, 87–138
    for students with disabilities, 52
    supplemental, 120, 121t
    technology, 89–103
    total staff, 120

Support staff
    natural, 120–122
    specialized, 120–122
    total, 120, 121t

Teacher-to-student ratios, 32
Teachers
    communication tools for, 134–138
    roles of, 10, 11t
Teams
    interdisciplinary, 107–108
    school, 24, 29–31
        cautionary notes for, 37
        collaborative, 27–40
        importance of, 39–40
        key components, 31–40
        model, 30f, 30–31
    student-based interdisciplinary
        teams, 109, 111t
Technology
    assistive, 101–102
    as bridge to accomplish specific
        activities, 97–98
    educational, 99
    example benefits of, 99–100
    example classroom with, 92–96,
        130–134
    guide for purchasing, 99
    high-tech adaptations, 91
    low-tech adaptations, 92–96
    resources, 102–103
    school district policies, responsi-
        bilities, and procedures,
        99–100
    to support belonging and achieve-
        ment, 89–103
    talented techies, 98
    as tool, 96
Technology-Related Assistance for
    Individuals with Disabilities
    Act of 1988 (PL 100-407), 99
Testing, 10, 11t
    accommodations for standardized
        achievement testing, 77, 78t
    tiered, 68
    as variable to change, 10, 11t
Text formats, alternative, 64
Tiered assignments and tests, 68

Time management, *see* Scheduling
Title I learners, 120
Total staff support, 120, 121*t*
Tutors, peer, 120, 121*t*

Unit planners, 55–59
Units of study
    central issues, problems, or questions, 46–47
    four-step process for creating, 49–52
    "grabbers" for, 47
    sample lesson plan, 55, 57*f*
    standards-based, 49
Universal design, 98

U.S. Department of Education, Office of Special Education and Rehabilitative Services (OSERS), 99

Vision, 21–22
Visual literacy, 64
Volunteers, community, 24–25

Web sites on assistive technology, 101–102
Weekly Assignment Sheets, 55–59, 58*f*
Writing
    holistic rubrics for, 79, 81*t*
    prompts and questions for, 67–68

Transform your classroom with two more books on inclusive schools!

Inclusive High Schools
Learning from Contemporary Classrooms

By Douglas Fisher, Ph.D., Caren Sax, Ed.D.,
& Ian Pumpian, Ph.D.

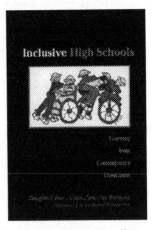

With inclusion advice from educators who've been there, this book provides a framework for developing inclusive high schools. It offers a detailed account of high schools that have struggled, strategized, and ultimately achieved successful inclusion. You'll learn how they built school-based relationships, developed support strategies, communicated responsibilities, prepared for the classroom, established continuity, planned lessons, adapted curricula, and redistributed school resources. You'll recognize common challenges to adopting inclusive practices and find proven strategies you can use in your school.

$27.00 • 1999 • 240 pages • 6 x 9 • paperback • ISBN 1-55766-379-3

Inclusive Urban Schools

Edited by Douglas Fisher, Ph.D., & Nancy Frey, Ph.D.

What are the particular challenges of inclusion in urban elementary, middle, or high schools—and how do educators successfully address them? Find out in this absorbing book, which uses nine in-depth case studies of actual city schools or districts to explore key issues in urban inclusive education. For each major city chapter, some of which are written by teachers and principals themselves, you'll

- examine how educators addressed a crucial topic in inclusion, such as early literacy instruction, diversity, peer relationships, access to the general curriculum, curricular adaptations, and transition

- discover practical ideas and lessons that you can use with students of varying grade levels and disabilities

- explore the history of the school's inclusion effort, diversity of their student body, and service delivery for their students with disabilities

- learn from the commentary of leading researchers, who expand on the lessons learned and provide information about implementing inclusive reforms

Whether you're in charge of a classroom, a school, or a whole system, you'll need this honest yet hopeful book to navigate the challenges of inclusive urban education.

$27.00 • 2004 • 288 pages • 6 x 9 • paperback • ISBN 1-55766-663-6

PLEASE SEND ME

___ *Inclusive High Schools* / Stock #3793 / $27.00
___ *Inclusive Middle Schools* / Stock #4862 / $27.00
___ *Inclusive Urban Schools* / Stock #6639 / $27.00
___ sets of *Inclusive High Schools & Inclusive Middle Schools* / Stock #5257 / $48.00

___ Check enclosed (payable in U.S.A. dollars to Brookes Publishing Co.)
___ Purchase Order attached (bill my institution)
___ Please charge my credit card:
    O American Express O MasterCard O Visa

Credit Card #: _____ Exp. Date: _____

Signature (required with credit card use):

_____

Name:

_____

Daytime Phone:

_____

Street Address:

_____ ❏ residential ❏ commercial
Complete street address required.

City/State/ZIP:

_____ Country: _____

E-mail Address:

_____

❏ Yes! I want to receive special web site discount offers! My e-mail address will not be shared with any other party.

Photocopy this form, and mail it to **Brookes Publishing Co.**, P.O. Box 10624,
Baltimore, MD 21285-0624, U.S.A.; FAX 410-337-8539; Call **1-800-638-3775**
(...M.–5 P.M., ET U.S.A. and CAN) or 410-337-9580 (worldwide);
or order online at **www.brookespublishing.com**

Shipping & Handling

For pretax total of	Add*	For CAN
$0.00 - $49.99	$5.00	$7.00
$50.00 - $69.99	10%	$7.00
$70.00 - $399.99	10%	10%
$400.00 and over	8%	8%

*calculate percentage on product total

Shipping rates are for UPS Ground Delivery within continental U.S.A. For other shipping options and rates, call 1-800-638-3775 (in the U.S.A. and CAN) and 410-337-9580 (worldwide).

Subtotal $ _____

5% sales tax, Maryland only + $ _____

7% business tax (GST), CAN only + $ _____

Shipping (see chart) + $ _____

Total (in U.S.A. dollars) = $ _____

Your list code is **BA 105**

All prices in U.S.A. dollars. Policies and prices subject to change without notice. Prices may be higher outside the U.S.A. You may return books within 30 days for a full credit of the product price. Refunds will be issued for prepaid orders. Items must be returned in resalable condition.

Browse our entire catalog, read excerpts, and find special offers at
www.brookespublishing.com